ACKNOWLEDGMENTS

Editorial Director: Erin Conley
Designers: Linda Davis of Star Type and Jeanette Miller
Special thanks to Suzanne Cracraft, Maria Llull, Kirsty Melville, Bob Moog,
Hillary Osness and Nancy Spector for their invaluable assistance.

This compilation © 2005 University Games.
Brainteasers © 2003 University Games, Symbol Simon © 2004
Bob Moog and University Games, Secret Identities © 2004 Bob Moog and
University Games, Opical Teasers © 2004 Al Seckel and University Games.

First edition published in 2005

Spinner Books, a division of

University Games Corporation
2030 Harrison Street San Francisco CA 94110

University Games Europe B.V.
Australielaan 52 6199 AA Maastricht Airport Netherlands

University Games Australia
10 Apollo Street Warriewood 2102 Australia

Library of Congress Cataloging-in-Publication Data on file with the publisher

ISBN: 1-57528-929-6

Printed in China

1 2 3 4 5 6 7 8 9 10 - 09 08 07 06 05

Table of Contents

3

Introduction

Welcome to the world of Armchair Puzzlers™. If we've been doing our jobs right, you've sat down with one of our little chairs before, ready to solve away. If not, well then, we're happy we've caught your eye and hope our puzzles will drive you mad for more.

The Armchair Puzzlers series started in 2003 when I gathered several of our top game inventors and asked them to share their favorite puzzles and create lots of fun and challenging new ones. This book is the tenth in the series and a great follow-up to our first edition of *The Overstuffed Book of Armchair Puzzlers.* It includes three sections written by me and one by my good friend, Al Seckel. *Brainteasers* will make you think while you chuckle. *Symbol Simon* is a collection of picture puzzles that I've created over the past 20 years. *Secret Identities* features a new type of word puzzle that tests your cultural IQ. Finally, Al's optical teasers are sure to confound you—and challenge your visual acuity.

We hope you're able to take some time to kick up your feet and enjoy our newest edition to the Armchair Puzzlers family.

Enjoy!
Bob Moog

BRAINTEASERS

5

Precedent or President

Is it more likely that Peter Cannon is an historian or an economist if he thinks that Abraham Lincoln is five times better than George Washington but four times worse than Andrew Jackson?

SOLUTIONS FOUND ON PAGE 216.

6

Alphabet Soup

What **three** letters can be arranged to describe

a beverage,
a verb
and
a homonym?

Armchair Puzzlers • Brainteasers

The circle game

Geometry is hard for Silly Sally.

Which is **BIGGER?**

a square with a 1 foot side

or

a circle with a 1 foot diameter?

SOLUTIONS FOUND ON PAGE 216.

7

Paw Paw's Handyman

Quincy can paint a room in 6 hours.

Emmitt can paint the same room in 3 hours.

How long will it take if they are both painting?

Armchair Puzzlers • Brainteasers

Panhandling

In addition to Florida, name 5 states with bulging and protruding peninsulas or panhandles.

SOLUTIONS FOUND ON PAGE 216.

8

Pied Piper Wanted

How many rats are in the room if there is a rat in each of the 4 corners and 3 rats across from every rat and a rat in the corner next to every rat?

Armchair Puzzlers · Brainteasers

The Disappearing Pickles

Peter Piper the pickle salesman went to market and sold half of his pickles plus half a pickle. He was left with one whole pickle. How many pickles did Peter Piper start with?

Blue Light Special

SOLUTIONS FOUND ON PAGE 216.

9

Three guys go into a hardware store, all looking to buy the same thing. William buys 1 for $1. Billy buys 99 for $2. Finally, Willie buys 757 for $3. What were they buying?

Armchair Puzzlers • Brainteasers

Lost in Space

In what state would you find yourself if you

left St. Louis and went five miles east, then

200 miles north and then

40 miles west?

5 mi
E ▷

200 mi
N △

40 mi
W ◁

SOLUTIONS FOUND ON PAGE 216.

10

over easy

Who am I?

I am a very fragile, rotund little man. I once had an accident that left me so disfigured that even the King of England and his fine staff failed at attempts to repair me.

Stand and Sign

I am from Ohio and I served as both leader of my country in the early 20th century and as a justice of my country's highest court. Baseball is my favorite sport and I made my greatest contribution to the game when I got tired of sitting around $7/9$ of the way through a game.

Who am I?

Wordly Wise

SOLUTIONS FOUND ON PAGE 216.

11

Alva's new Ford Fiesta was towed while sitting in front of this sign. Why did Alva go to court to fight the ticket? Why did Alva bring Mr. Smith, a local high school teacher, with him as his witness?

No
Unauthorized
Vehicles
Will Be Towed

Food, Please

Napoleon's army was the first to use what food preservative device in combat?

SOLUTIONS FOUND ON PAGE 216.

12

Hint: Napoleon knew that "an army travels on its stomach."

Winter Construction

Lani's hands were freezing after building a snowman without any gloves. Should Lani warm up by putting her hands under cold water or hot water?

Most Wanted ?

In which state capitals will you find these guys?

Al

Jeff

Sal

Harris

No Blankety Blanks!

Look at the words below and see if you can complete the statement by filling in the blanks. A word hidden inside of each word listed below is needed to complete the sentence.

SOLUTIONS FOUND ON PAGE 216.

13

A. Panhandle
   Spearmint
   Aspirin

B. Wheeling
   Germany
   Washington

A. Meg stopped the _____ with a quick stab of the _____ that she held with her right _____ .

B. The _____ was really tired since the _____ weighed a _____ .

Armchair Puzzlers • Brainteasers

Light Show

What is the name of the toy constructed by placing multiple mirrors at different angles and shooting light through a tube, bouncing the light from one mirror to the next?

SOLUTIONS FOUND ON PAGE 216.

14

Color Blind

1 Major League Baseball umpire's underwear

2 A Catholic novice's garb

3 Archie Andrew's hair

4 Stitching on a baseball

5 Wimbledon tennis players' dress code

Is it black, red or white?

Armchair Puzzlers • Brainteasers

Family Matters

True **False**

In 14 states, including Utah, it is legal for a man to marry his widow's sister.

Dog Dayz

What is the next letter in this series?

D N O S A J

Armchair Puzzlers • Brainteasers

Just Kidding

"Let's go play with the 3 kids up on that hill," said Silly Sally. Joe ran ahead but only found 2 children and some grazing farm animals when he arrived. Where did the third kid go?

SOLUTIONS FOUND ON PAGE 217.

16

Buried Treasure

Is it against the law to bury a person in Utah who is permanently living in Nevada?

Utah

Go West, Young Woman

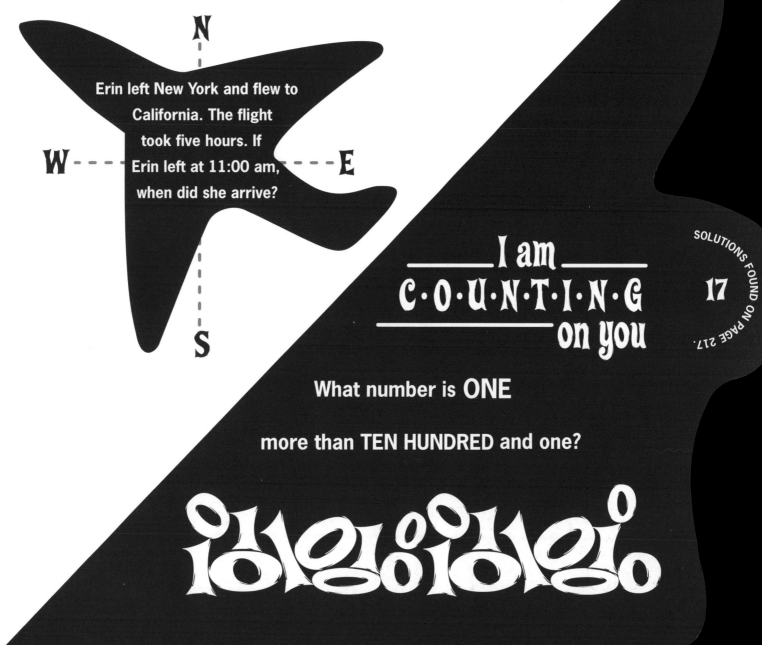

N

W – – – – – – – – – **E**

S

Erin left New York and flew to California. The flight took five hours. If Erin left at 11:00 am, when did she arrive?

_____ I am _____
C·O·U·N·T·I·N·G
_____ on you

What number is **ONE**

more than **TEN HUNDRED** and one?

SOLUTIONS FOUND ON PAGE 217.

Armchair Puzzlers · Brainteasers

All in the Family

Try to name the three most closely related pairs of presidents.

SOLUTIONS FOUND ON PAGE 217.

18

Hysterical History

Did the Germans bomb Pearl Harbor on December 7th

1941,

1942

or

1944?

Sister Sprinters

Nina and Lydia start from their home and each run 2 miles. Nina can run a mile in 8 minutes 30 seconds and Lydia can run a mile in 9 minutes 10 seconds. When they finish running, what is the farthest apart they can be?

Sunrise, Sunset

SOLUTIONS FOUND ON PAGE 217.

19

What starts today,

can't be found at noon

and is required to end sunset?

Digestive Detective

Jeff and Vinnie met for dinner at Fitz's Fine Foods. After they both went to the bathroom they sat down and ordered. The waiter described the special as trout almondine with asparagus covered in hollandaise sauce. Jeff said, "I'll take it, but Vinnie wants something else. He had asparagus for lunch."

How did Jeff know what Vinnie had for lunch?

SOLUTIONS FOUND ON PAGE 217.

20

3 Men and a Lady

Melissa went to dinner with
Andrew,
George
and
Ulysses,
but she ate **alone**.

Not surprisingly, they all showed up to pay for her meal. **Why?**

Can YOU canoe?

TWO fathers and TWO sons went on a canoe trip,

ONE fell out

and TWO were left.
Where is the 4th man?

Ben Cartwright rode into Virginia City late on Friday. Ben Cartwright stayed two days, but still rode out on Friday.

Explain.

SOLUTIONS FOUND ON PAGE 217.

It's Not Over–Till It's Over

Andrew and John are professional tennis players who never like to lose. They were 9/10 of the way through a game with John down by 3 points. Andrew made a very good shot. Then, without giving John a chance, Andrew made another good shot. John suspected that he was going to lose, even though the game wasn't over. Why?

SOLUTIONS FOUND ON PAGE 217.

22

Coin - cidentally

Miss Korn collected coins and referred to her coin collection by nicknames. Her pennies were the Cu collection; her nickels were the Ni collection. What did Miss Korn call her collection of silver dollars?

Phractured Phrases

Try to identify the two words we replaced
in these well-known quotes below:

"What is good for the stomach is
good for the complexion."

"In this world nothing is certain
but franks and beans."

"You're either part of the infield
or part of the outfield."

"The only thing we have to
drink is beer itself."

Road Trip

Which state capitals
would you visit to find a. . .

ram

cord

bus

dove

SOLUTIONS FOUND ON PAGE 217.

23

Armchair Puzzlers • Brainteasers

Talking States

What did Flora-di of?

What did Tenna see?

What did Della wear?

SOLUTIONS FOUND ON PAGE 217.

24

Sheila the GREAT

Sheila lives in Chicago. One night she sat down for dinner with the window open and heard a gunshot. Then she witnessed two gruesome deaths. Before she could leave the room she saw a building catch fire. Why didn't Sheila call the police?

Armchair Puzzlers • Brainteasers

Nuts to You

1. What is the largest nut?

2. What is a policeman's favorite nut?

3. What is another name for a sneeze nut?

Wait Until Dark

SOLUTIONS FOUND ON PAGE 218.

25

Jacob and Lutz were camping in June. Before going to sleep they decided to read a book. They both agreed to stop reading when it got dark. They were not fast readers, but they both finished the entire encyclopedia. How?

Armchair Puzzlers • Brainteasers

Drink Up

What city in Thailand would you visit to order an original Singapore Sling?

SOLUTIONS FOUND ON PAGE 218.

26

A Bush in the Hand

Would you be more likely to find 2 bushes and no trees at...

Disneyland

the White House lawn,

or

the Supreme Court building?

Armchair Puzzlers • Brainteasers

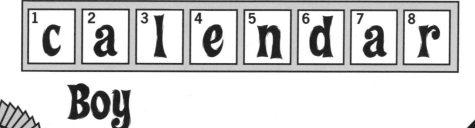

calendar Boy

Jupiter Jones won a contest where first prize was "use of a Rolls Royce with chauffeur for 30 days of 24 hours each." He used the limousine on June 1, 2 and 3, for 8 hours each day. He then used it again from June 12 to June 19 for 8 hours each day. When Jupiter arrived to take the limo on July 2 he was told that his 30 days were up. Why did Jupiter disagree and how many days did he think were left?

Sunny and Fair

SOLUTIONS FOUND ON PAGE 218.

27

Who am I?

I am a singer who has had hits in five consecutive decades. I also have won an Academy Award.® I am as well-known for my Bob Mackie dresses as I am for my songs. In 2003 I began my "farewell" concert tour.

Armchair Puzzlers • Brainteasers

Down Under

Shane bet Steve that it was impossible to go back in time.

Why did Shane agree that Steve won the bet when their plane arrived in Los Angeles, California from Adelaide, Australia?

SOLUTIONS FOUND ON PAGE 218.

28

Double Trouble

!

Pacific Ocean

Atlantic Ocean

In what U.S. city can you visit a state capital, see the Atlantic Ocean, drive an hour to the Pacific Ocean and see 17th-century architecture?

Birthday Boy

Horace Jordan was born in February 1896. Why did he only celebrate his first birthday in 1904?

SOLUTIONS FOUND ON PAGE 218.

29

Shoe Who?

Silly Sally was so excited to fly from San Francisco to London that she forgot how sore her new shoes made her feet. She took her shoes off as soon as she was settled in her seat. When the plane landed 10 hours later, Sally started screaming at the flight attendant when she realized that her shoes had shrunk. **Explain.**

Armchair Puzzlers • Brainteasers

Friend or Fiend?

If Billy the Brat told Silly Sally

"I hate you,
I loathe you,
I despise you."

Would he be a practitioner of

hyperbole,
redundancy or
immaturity?

SOLUTIONS FOUND ON PAGE 218.

30

Time to Go

Mr. Rosner walked into the room and noticed Silly Sally sitting patiently on the floor reading a magazine. Mr. Rosner's alarm clock was totally destroyed and parts were all over the room. What had Silly Sally been up to?

Forgotten Children

Homer's mother has four children.

Three of them are named
Spring,
Summer
and
Autumn.

What is the fourth named?

Epitome

Jeff Glik is camping outside Bemidji, Minnesota with only oil lamps, a candle and some birch bark. He has only one match. Which should he light first?

SOLUTIONS FOUND ON PAGE 218.

31

BUS STOP

125

If 50 kids fit in a school bus, how many buses do you need to get 125 kids to school?

SOLUTIONS FOUND ON PAGE 218.

32

Happy Birthday, Granny

Claudia and her 52-year-old mother went to her grandmother's 50th birthday party together. How can Claudia's grandmother be younger than Claudia's mother?

Armchair Puzzlers • Brainteasers

Wide Load

Mr. Stone's truck attempted to enter a parking garage, but got caught underneath the garage ceiling because of the truck's 6'6" height. It won't budge forward or backward. How can he get the truck out from under the garage ceiling?

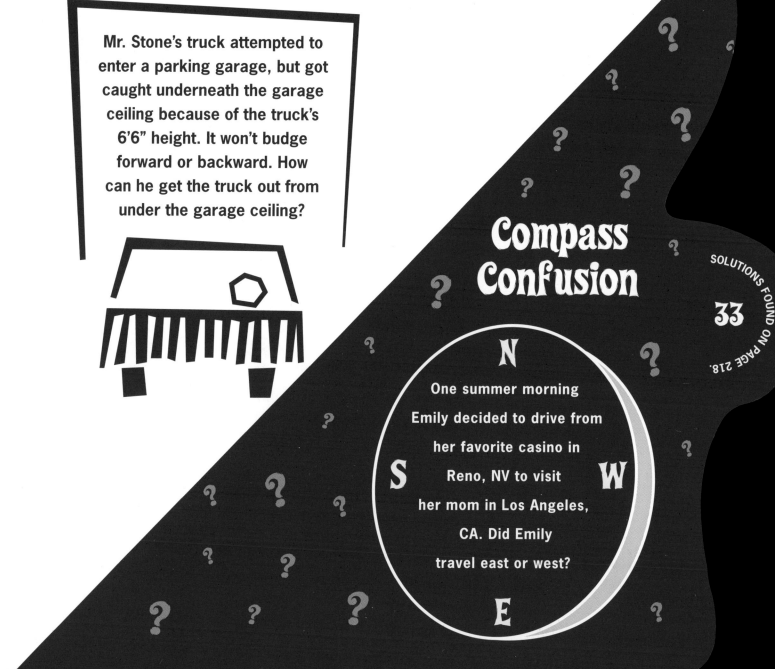

Compass Confusion

SOLUTIONS FOUND ON PAGE 218.

33

N

One summer morning Emily decided to drive from her favorite casino in Reno, NV to visit her mom in Los Angeles, CA. Did Emily travel east or west?

S

W

E

Armchair Puzzlers • Brainteasers

Cassie's Classic Conundrum

Using the digits 1 through 9, number the squares below so the sum of all the squares vertically, horizontally and diagonally is always 15.

(By the way, you can only use each number one time.)

SOLUTIONS FOUND ON PAGE 218.

Desperate Date

Name the European cities where Silly Sally went to find the following boys:

Don

Lin

Bud

Ari

(Hint: She went to Toronto to find Ron.)

Armchair Puzzlers • Brainteasers

Phone Tree

Maia wants to call all 10 kids in her 6th grade class

and then have each of them talk to each of the others.

What is the minimum number of conversations that will take place?

Fractional Sense

How much is 30 divided by 1/2 plus 3?

How do you represent the number 50 in base 5?

SOLUTIONS FOUND ON PAGE 219.

Armchair Puzzlers · Brainteasers

Busybody

A woman married **over 50 men** without ever getting divo rced. None of the men died and no one thought that she acted improperly.

Why?

SOLUTIONS FOUND ON PAGE 219.

36

E·X·T·R·A Credit

What two European cities would you visit to find Ed and Sara?

Sara

Ed

Armchair Puzzlers • Brainteasers

Chirp Chirp

What do the following birds have in common?

cardinals

ravens

eagles

falcons

If I Ran the ZOO

SOLUTIONS FOUND ON PAGE 219.

37

In what northern hemisphere city can you find indigenous tigers and lions?

Armchair Puzzlers • Brainteasers

No Blankety Blanks!

Look at the words below and see if you can complete the statement by filling in the blanks. A word hidden inside of each place listed below is needed to complete the sentence.

Broadway
Oregon
Kentucky
Frankfort
Colorado

The _____ of the _____

sent _____ and _____

on the wrong _____ .

SOLUTIONS FOUND ON PAGE 219.

38

Time is UP

I like time,
　　　　but I don't like clocks.

I like wine,
　　　　but I don't like beer.

I like Cherie,
　　　　but I don't like Jenny.

Do I like George, Bob or Mark?

Life's Lessons

What is it that you *need* to have life,

you won't have with death

and you can't start fun without?

The Getaway

SOLUTIONS FOUND ON PAGE 219.

39

Matt Brooks often goes the wrong way on a one-way street— PAST a police station. How does he get away with it without ever breaking the law?

Armchair Puzzlers • Brainteasers

Riddle Me This

I sizzle like bacon.
I'm made with an egg.
I've got lots of backbone,
but not even one leg.
I peel like an onion,
yet still remain whole.
I'm long like a fishpole,
but fit in a hole.

What am I?

SOLUTIONS FOUND ON PAGE 219.

40

Exciting

Hey, genius!
I start with the letter E.
I end with the letter E.
I usually contain one letter.
But I am not the letter E.

What am I?

EEE

Armchair Puzzlers · Brainteasers

I'm Never Blue

Sometimes I'm green,
sometimes I'm black.
When I'm yellow,
I'm a very nice fellow.
That's when I'm feeling
mighty a-peeling.

What am I?

Who Was That Masked Man?

SOLUTIONS FOUND ON PAGE 219.

41

Elizabeth has been working hard and she wants to go home. The masked man won't let her.

Why?

Weighing In

Betsy doesn't like to tell her weight. But she does like to create riddles. How much does Betsy weigh if her weight equals 50 lbs. plus half of her weight?

SOLUTIONS FOUND ON PAGE 219.

42

Roll Out the Barrel

Rick Tuttle is asked to carry a barrel of water across the desert for his Cub Scout troop. The barrel is 2 feet high, 1.5 feet in diameter and it weighs 100 pounds. What can he add to it to make it lighter?

Sum-thing's Up

The sum is 12 and the same digit is used three times to create the sum. Since the digit is not four, what is the digit?

Fur Sure

SOLUTIONS FOUND ON PAGE 219.

43

Scientists have found that cats are furrier on one side than the other. The side with the most fur is the side that cats most often lie on. Which side of a cat has more fur?

Armchair Puzzlers • Brainteasers

Touching Allowed

Hey, what's up?
They don't touch when you say "TOUCH"
—but they *do* touch when you say "SEPARATE."

What are they?

SOLUTIONS FOUND ON PAGE 219.

44

Lonely Nights

Slick Sam tried to enter the

nightclub but

was turned away

because it was full

of people. Yet Slick Sam

could tell there wasn't a single

person in there. **How is this possible?**

Armchair Puzzlers · Brainteasers

Change of Heart

Rick Holmstrom has something that he tried to avoid for a long time. But now that he's got it, he doesn't want to lose it.

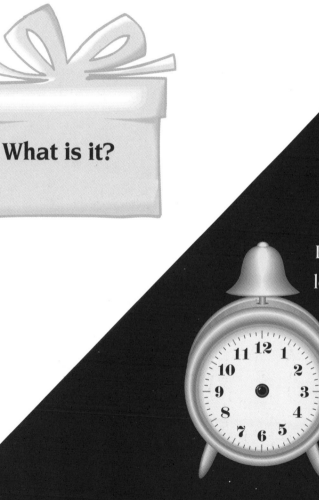

What is it?

Time's Up!

SOLUTIONS FOUND ON PAGE 219.

45

Little Ben is in London. He looks up at a clock. The big hand and the little hand are midway between 1 and 2, lying on top of each other. What time is it?

Freezer Burn

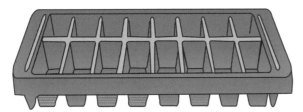

What did Chris the Confused pull out of the freezer and proudly offer to his hungry father for dessert?

SOLUTIONS FOUND ON PAGE 219.

46

SSSSSSS

What word becomes plural when an "s" is added, but becomes singular again by adding another "s"?

Armchair Puzzlers · Brainteasers

Symbol Simon

47

INSTRUCTIONS:

Each page in this section has its own "Symbol Simon" puzzle.
Sound out symbols and pictures to figure out what they mean.

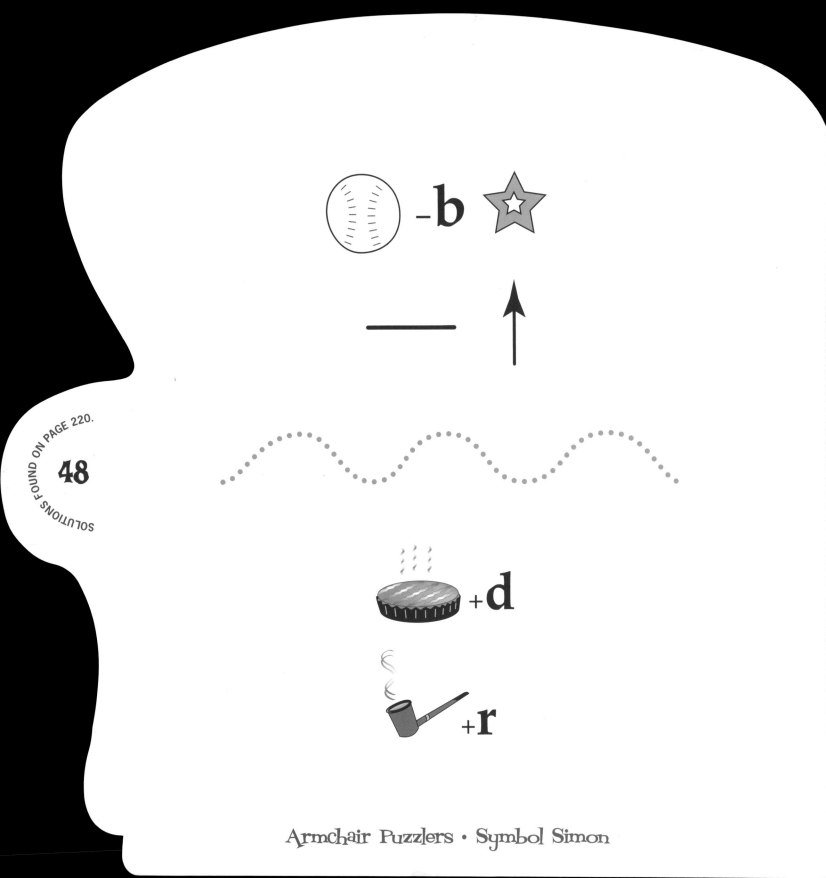

SOLUTIONS FOUND ON PAGE 220.

Armchair Puzzlers • Symbol Simon

 +re+

j+

 +r+

SOLUTIONS FOUND ON PAGE 220.

49

Armchair Puzzlers · Symbol Simon

t +

the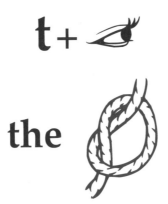

 + t +

SOLUTIONS FOUND ON PAGE 220.

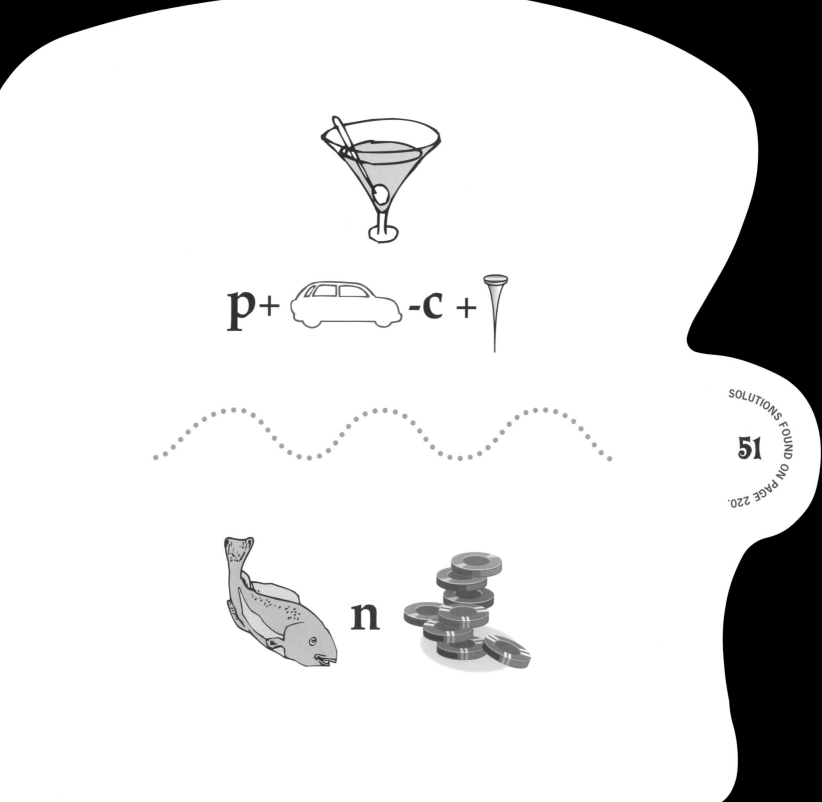

SOLUTIONS FOUND ON PAGE 220.

51

Armchair Puzzlers • Symbol Simon

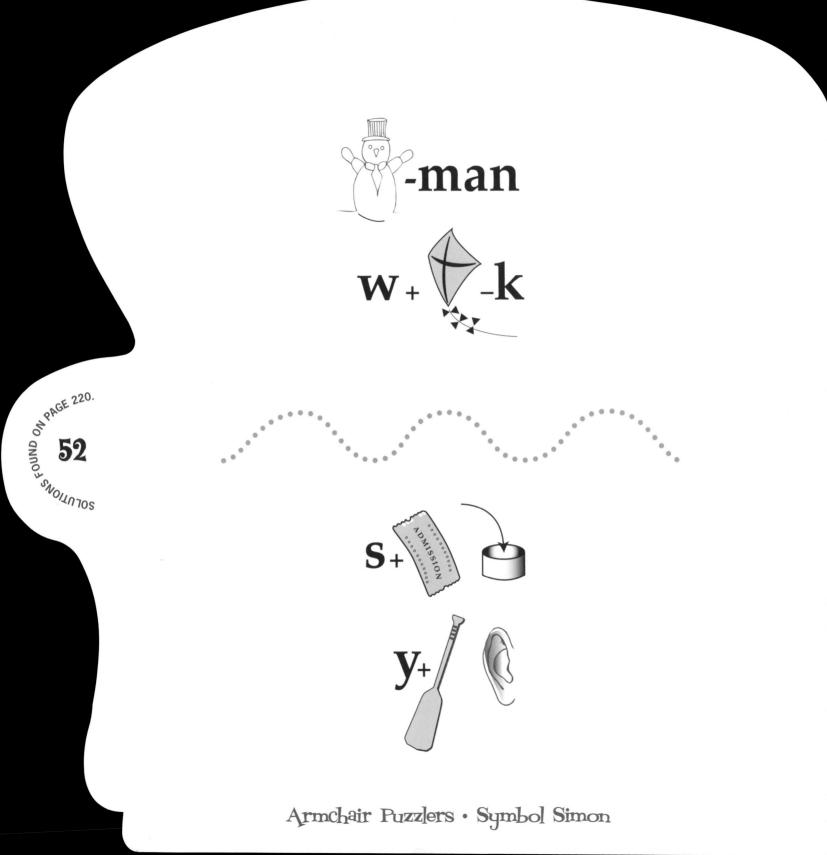

 +ing

 n

 +L

e+

SOLUTIONS FOUND ON PAGE 220.

Armchair Puzzlers • Symbol Simon

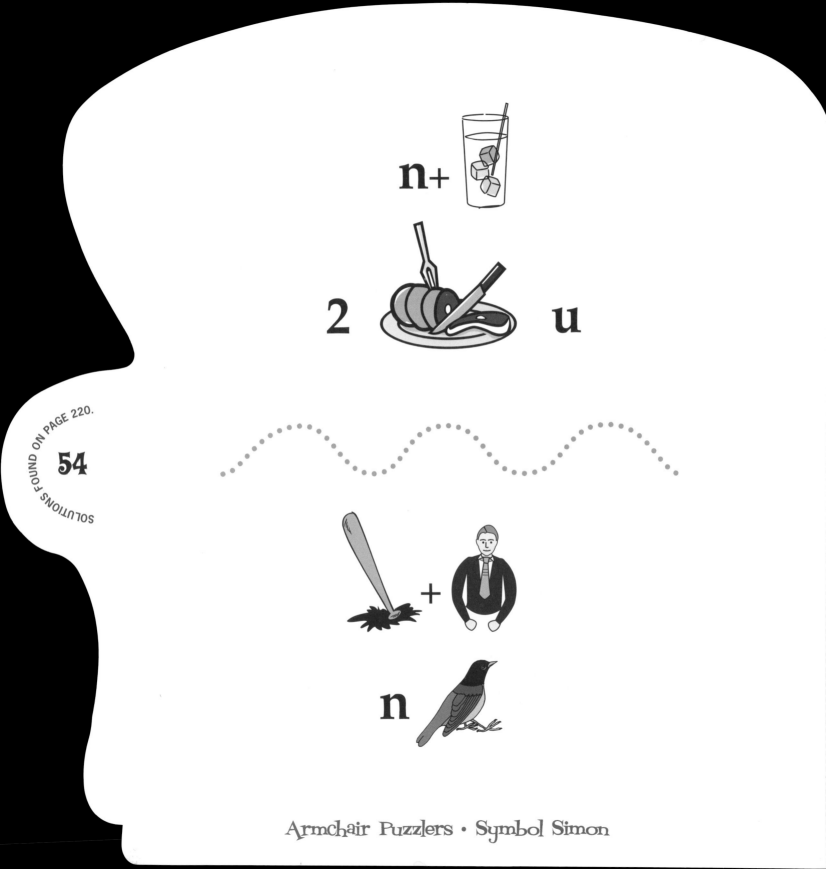

SOLUTIONS FOUND ON PAGE 220.

54

Armchair Puzzlers • Symbol Simon

2 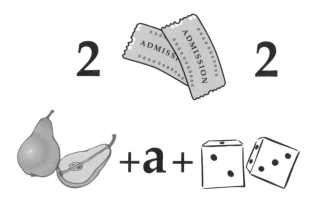 2

SOLUTIONS FOUND ON PAGE 220.

55

Armchair Puzzlers • Symbol Simon

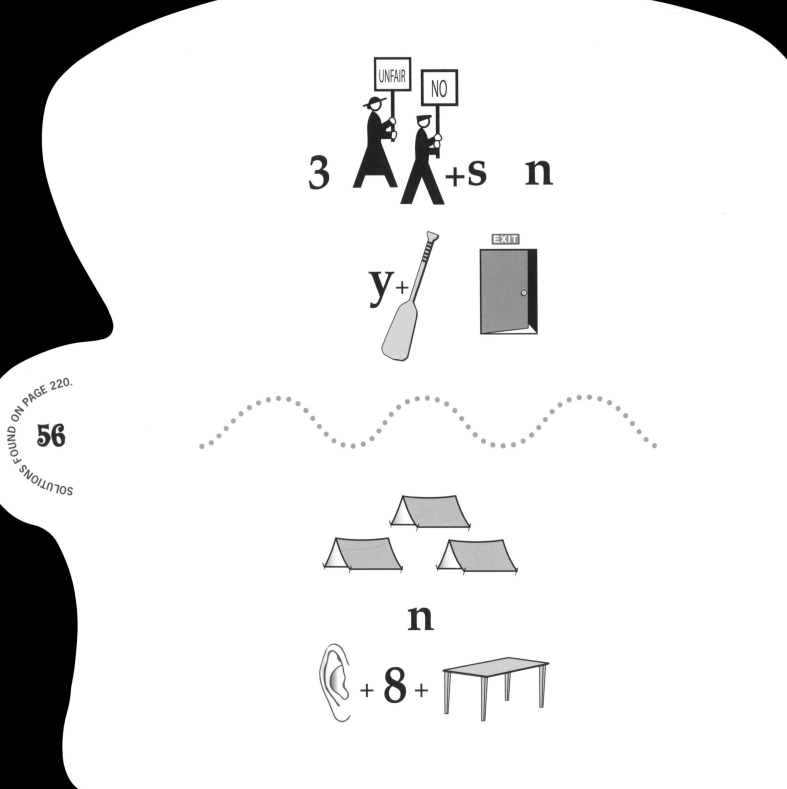

SOLUTIONS FOUND ON PAGE 220.

56

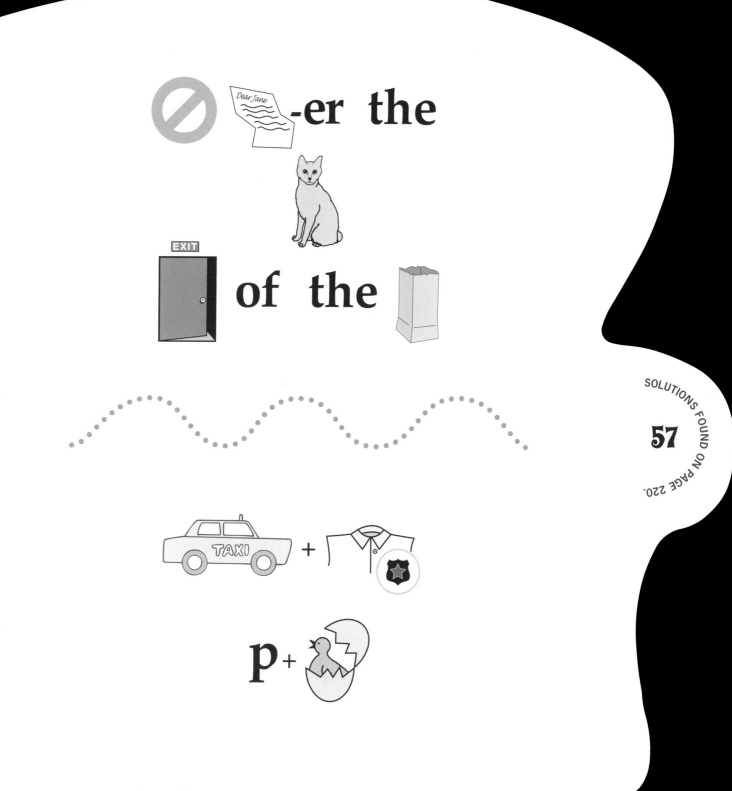

SOLUTIONS FOUND ON PAGE 220.

57

Armchair Puzzlers · Symbol Simon

SOLUTIONS FOUND ON PAGE 220.

58

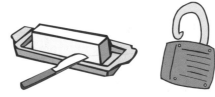

S +  + a

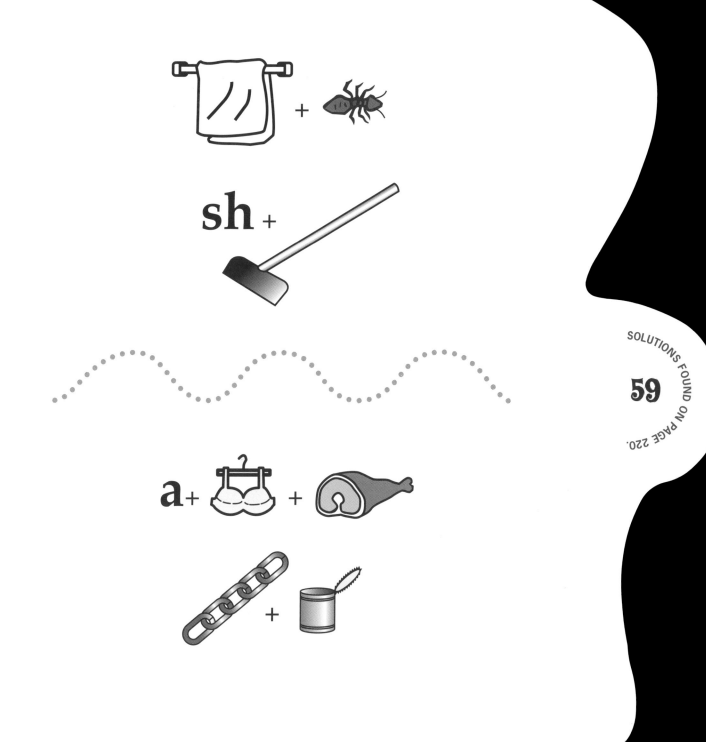

SOLUTIONS FOUND ON PAGE 220.

59

Armchair Puzzlers · Symbol Simon

of the

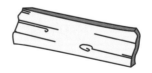 **+ a + 10**

SOLUTIONS FOUND ON PAGE 220.

60

Armchair Puzzlers • Symbol Simon

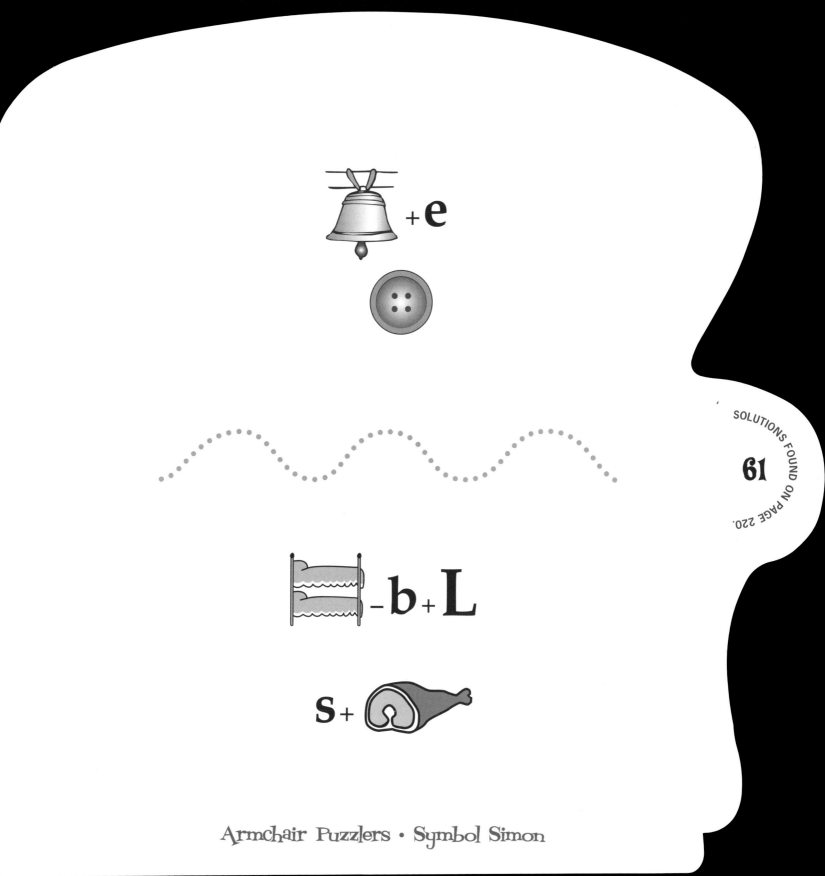

SOLUTIONS FOUND ON PAGE 220.

Armchair Puzzlers · Symbol Simon

SOLUTIONS FOUND ON PAGE 220.

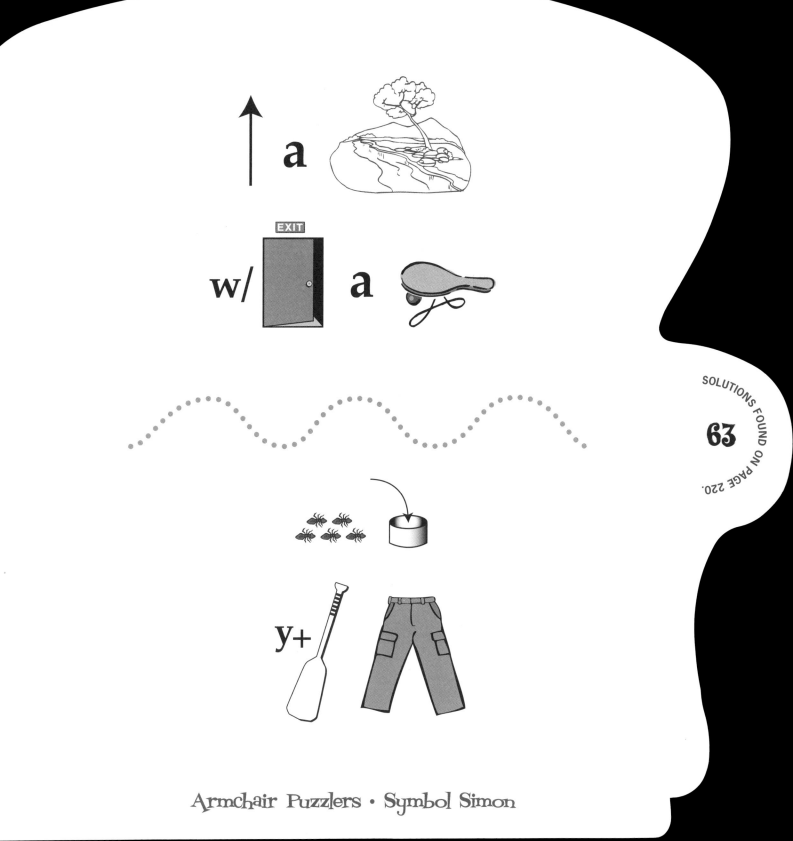

SOLUTIONS FOUND ON PAGE 220.

63

Armchair Puzzlers · Symbol Simon

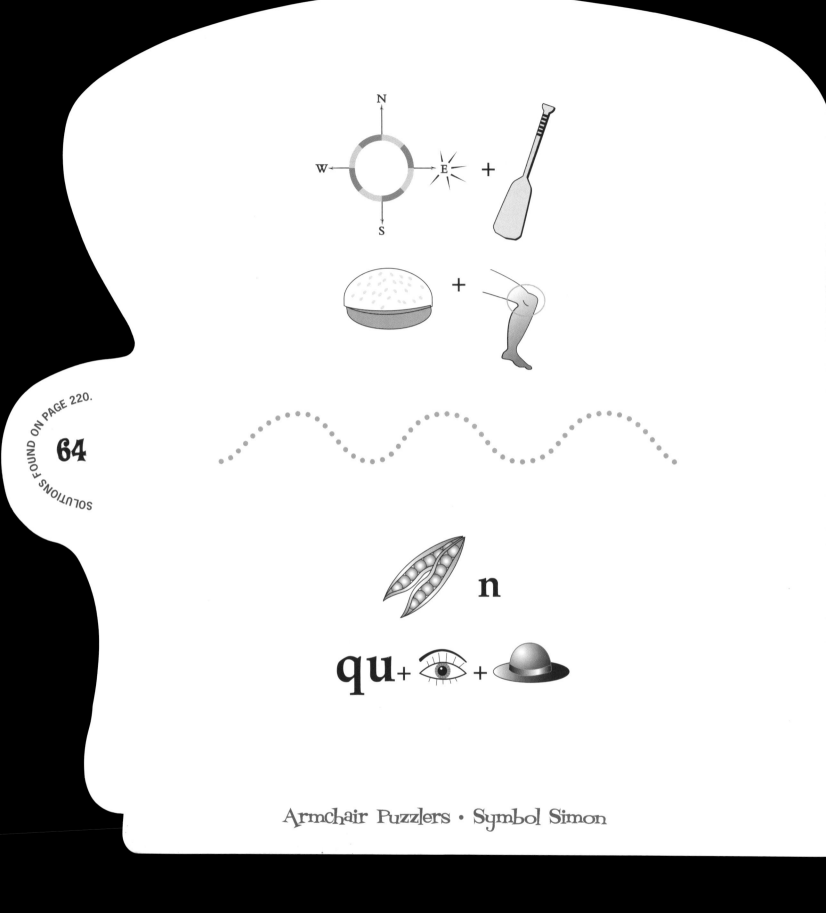

Armchair Puzzlers · Symbol Simon

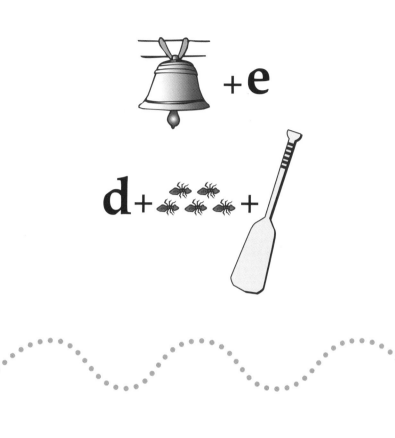

SOLUTIONS FOUND ON PAGE 220.

Armchair Puzzlers · Symbol Simon

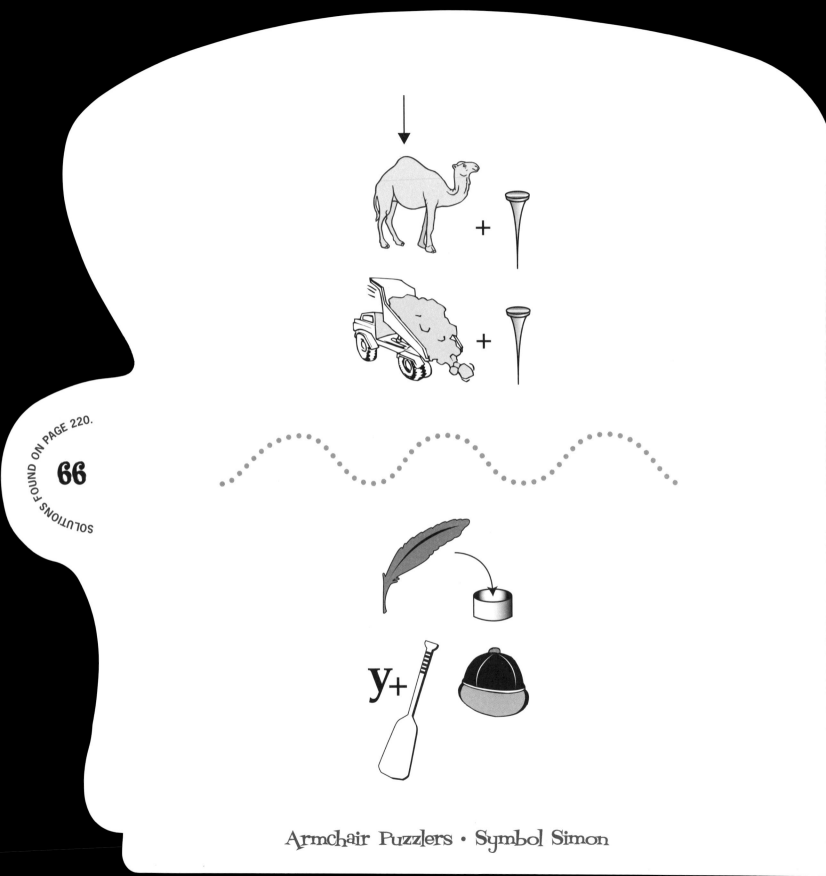

SOLUTIONS FOUND ON PAGE 220.

66

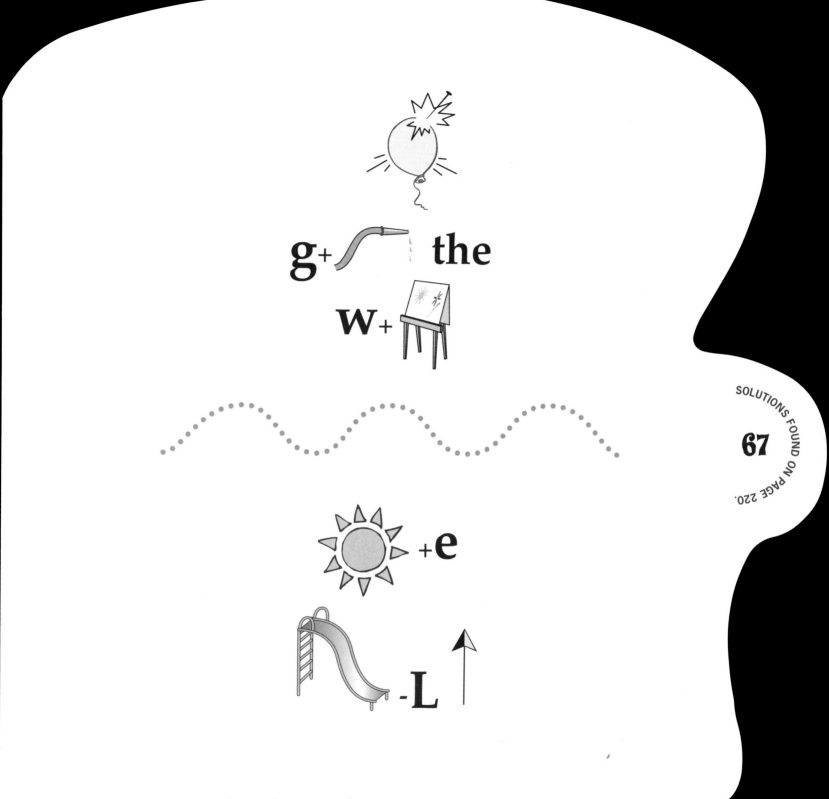

SOLUTIONS FOUND ON PAGE 220.

Armchair Puzzlers · Symbol Simon

SOLUTIONS FOUND ON PAGE 220.

L + 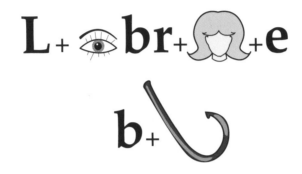 br + +e

b +

b + + the

SOLUTIONS FOUND ON PAGE 221.

Armchair Puzzlers · Symbol Simon

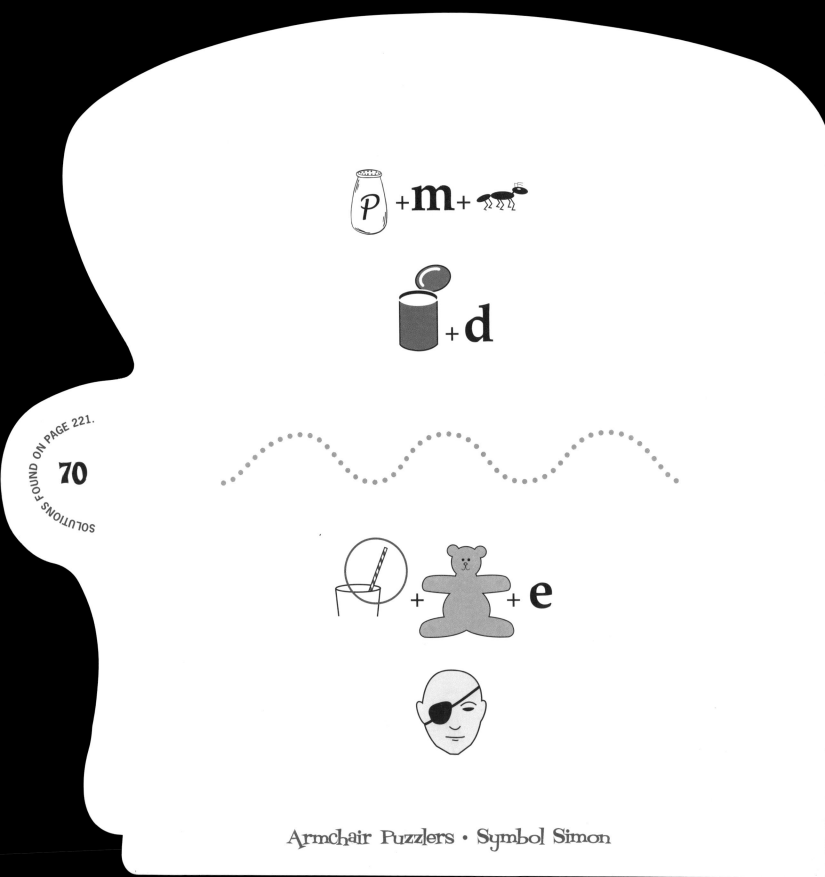

SOLUTIONS FOUND ON PAGE 221.

Armchair Puzzlers • Symbol Simon

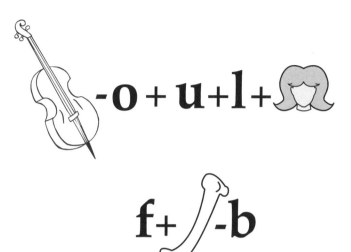-o+u+l+

f+ -b

-g

+r H+  -c

SOLUTIONS FOUND ON PAGE 221.

Armchair Puzzlers • Symbol Simon

SOLUTIONS FOUND ON PAGE 221.

m + ⌡ + **L** + ▢ -**band**

pr + 👁 + 🛶 + **e** + ⊤

thr+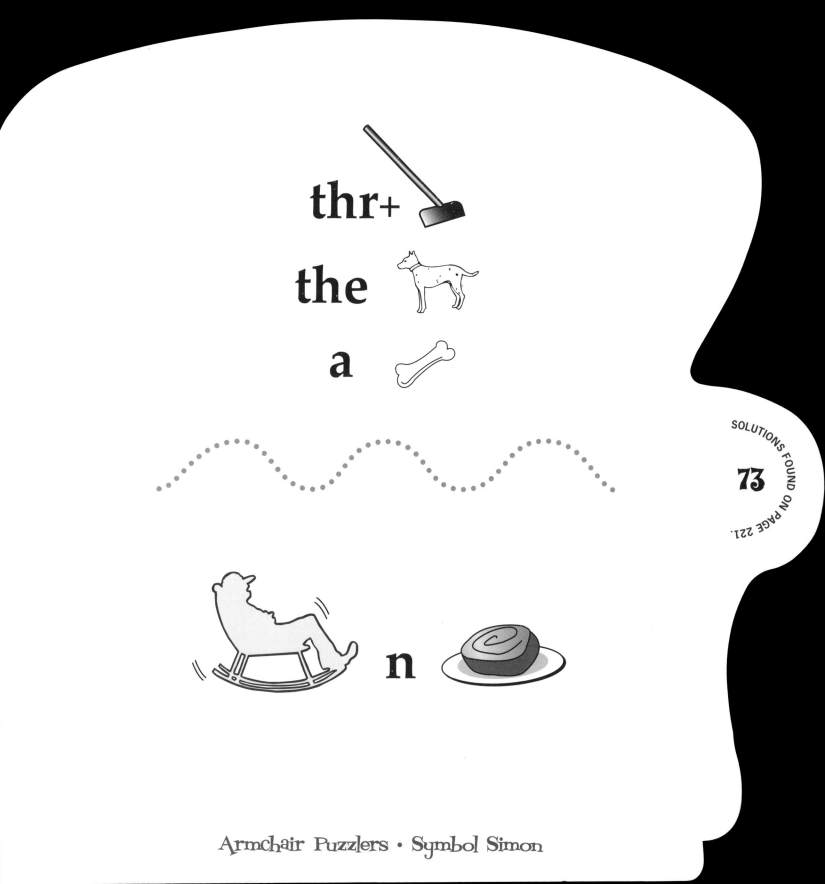

the

a

n

SOLUTIONS FOUND ON PAGE 221.

73

Armchair Puzzlers • Symbol Simon

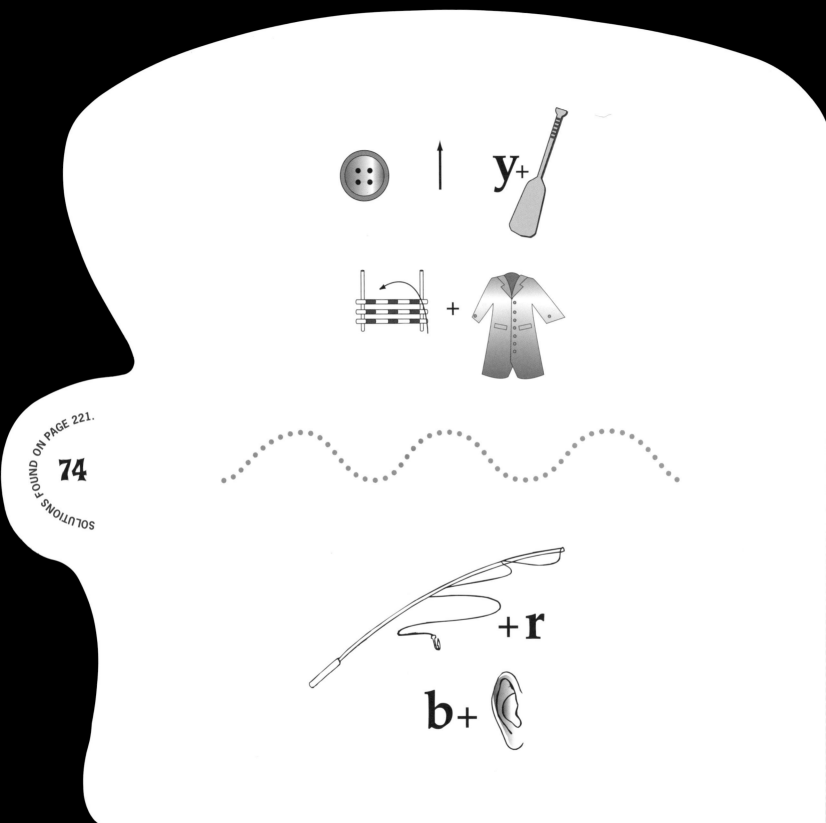

SOLUTIONS FOUND ON PAGE 221.

74

Armchair Puzzlers • Symbol Simon

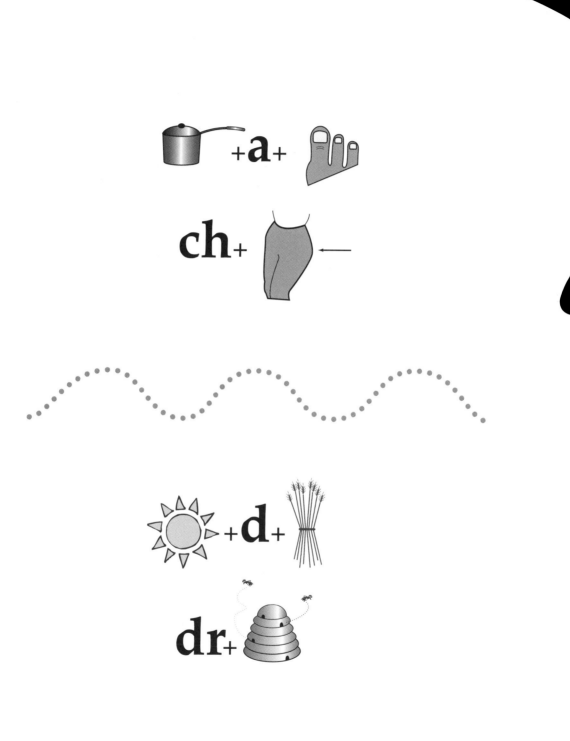

+a+

ch+ ←

SOLUTIONS FOUND ON PAGE 221.

+d+

dr+

SOLUTIONS FOUND ON PAGE 221.

t+ -r

the n

dr+ n

m+ +e

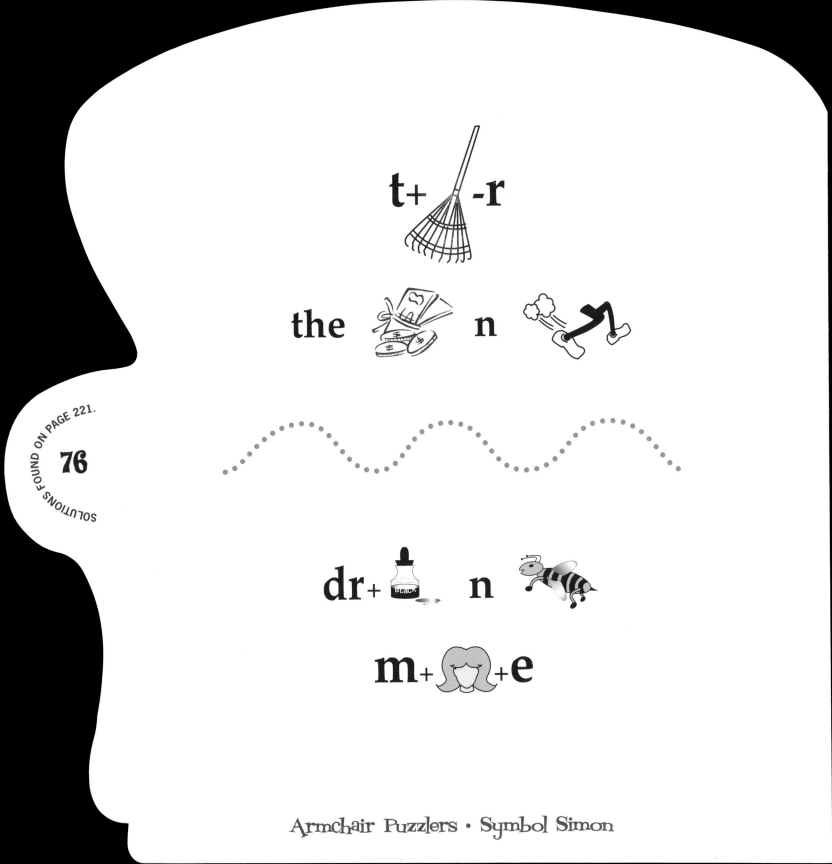

Armchair Puzzlers · Symbol Simon

 **y+**

thr+  **-g**

m+ 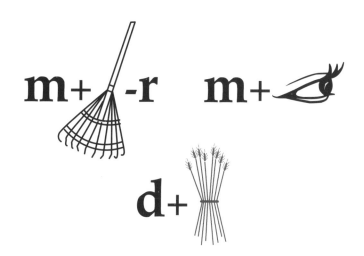 **-r   m+**

d+

SOLUTIONS FOUND ON PAGE 221.

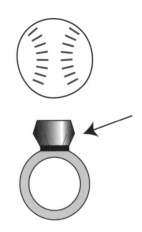

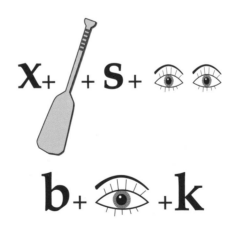

X + ✂ + **S** + 👁 👁

b + 👁 + **k**

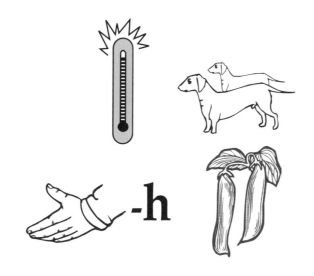

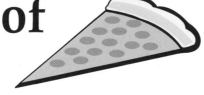

SOLUTIONS FOUND ON PAGE 221.

79

Armchair Puzzlers · Symbol Simon

SOLUTIONS FOUND ON PAGE 221.

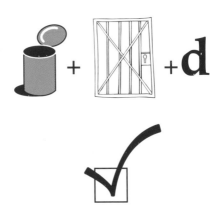 +d

L + v +  -k

 +e

Armchair Puzzlers • Symbol Simon

w+  a

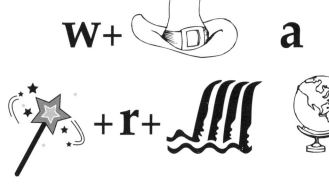 +r+

SOLUTIONS FOUND ON PAGE 221.

81

+k +

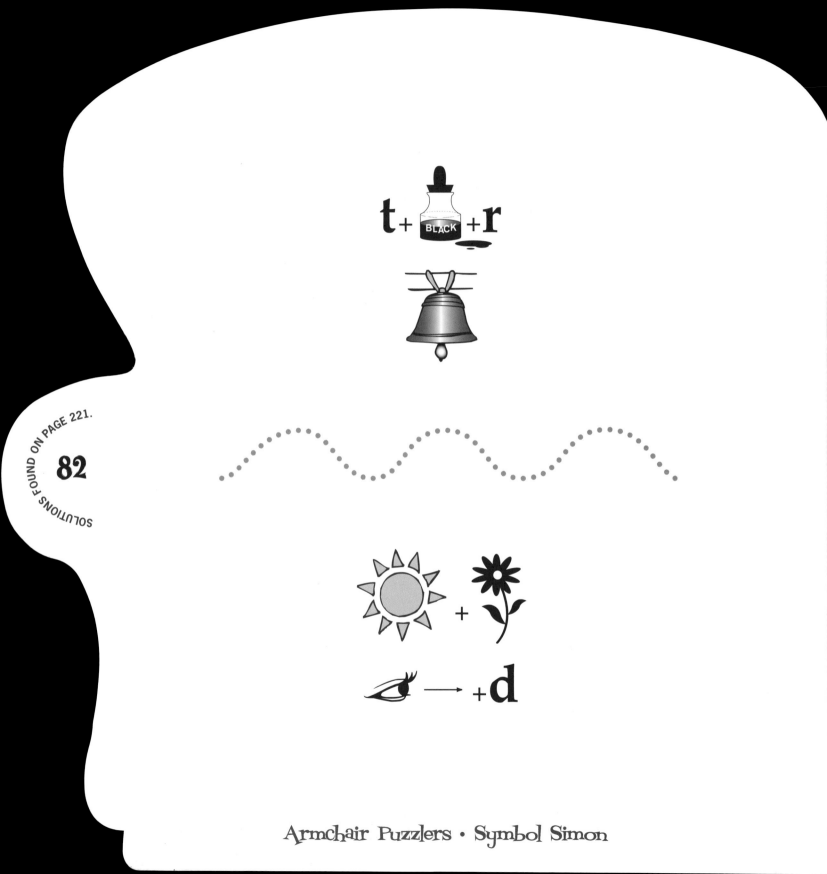

SOLUTIONS FOUND ON PAGE 221.

82

Armchair Puzzlers · Symbol Simon

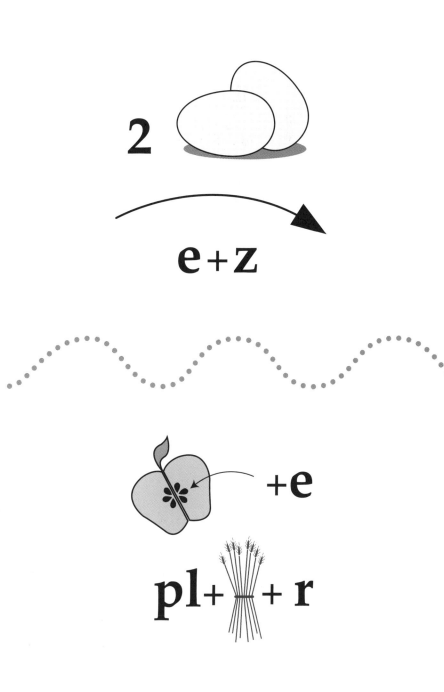

2 🥚

e+z

🍎 +e

pl+🌾+r

SOLUTIONS FOUND ON PAGE 221.

Armchair Puzzlers · Symbol Simon

SOLUTIONS FOUND ON PAGE 221.

Armchair Puzzlers · Symbol Simon

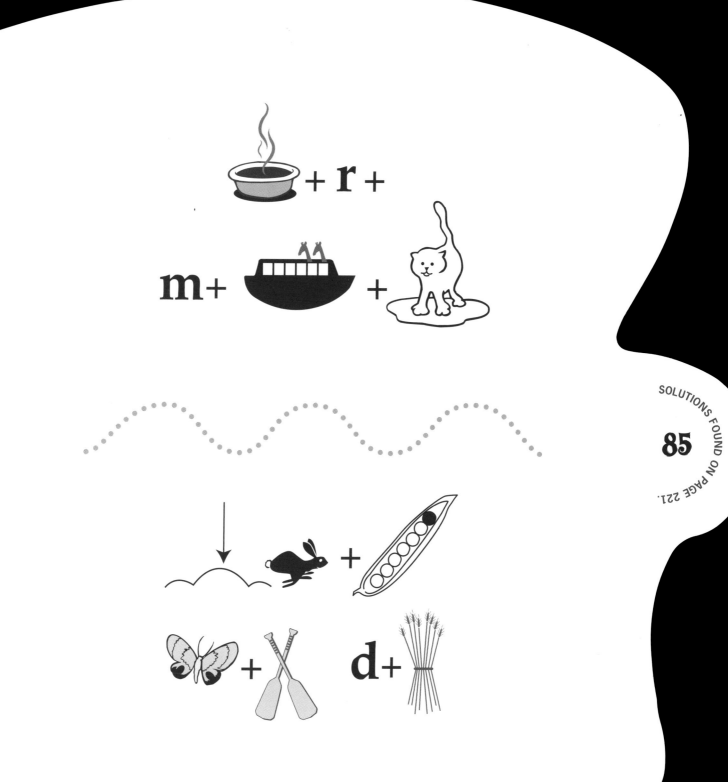

SOLUTIONS FOUND ON PAGE 221.

85

Armchair Puzzlers · Symbol Simon

SOLUTIONS FOUND ON PAGE 221.

$$10 + s$$
$$n + e \quad 1$$

Armchair Puzzlers • Symbol Simon

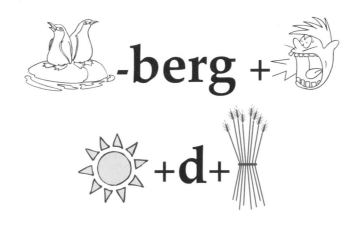 -berg +

 +d+

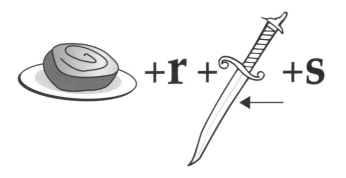 +r + +s

SOLUTIONS FOUND ON PAGE 221.

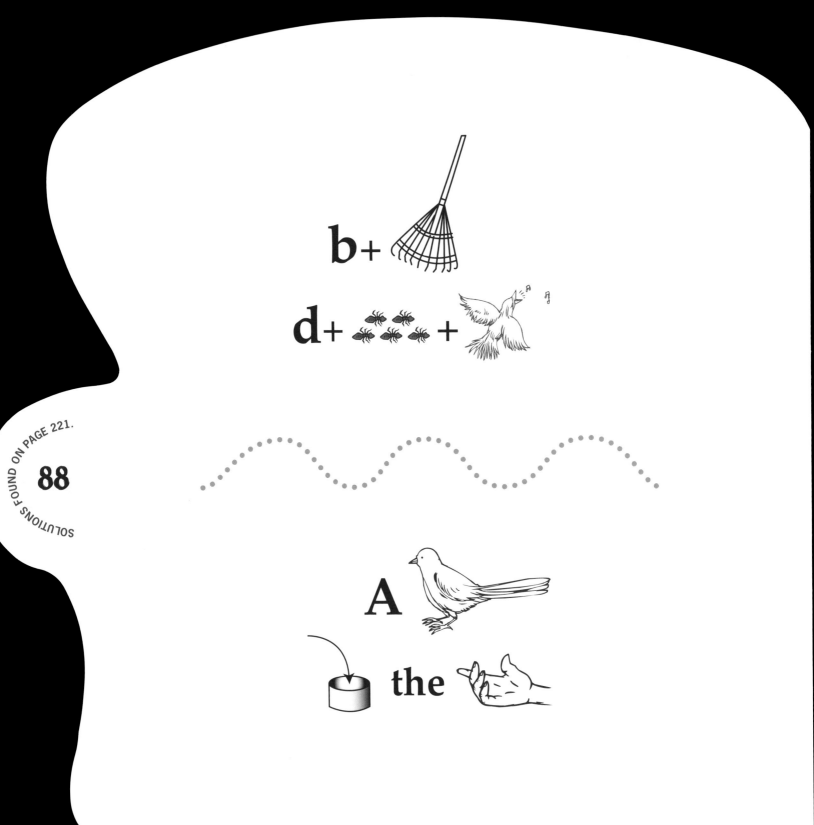

SOLUTIONS FOUND ON PAGE 221.

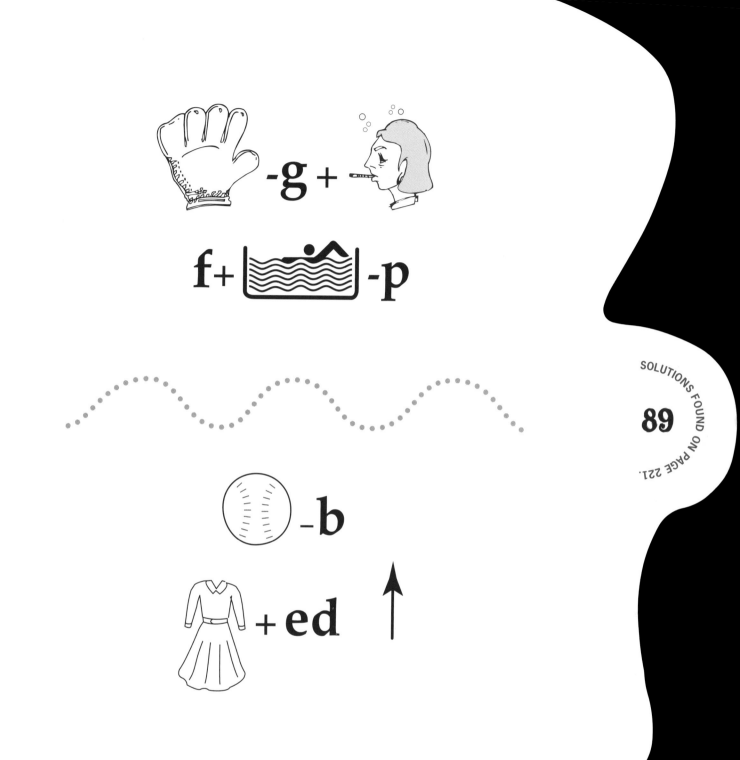

SOLUTIONS FOUND ON PAGE 221.

89

Armchair Puzzlers · Symbol Simon

 + Q

 + f

b +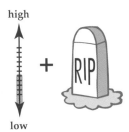

high

low + RIP

SOLUTIONS FOUND ON PAGE 221.

Armchair Puzzlers · Symbol Simon

Secret Identities

INSTRUCTIONS

Each page in this section has its own "Secret Identities" puzzle.

There are three types of puzzles: Get a Clue, Mysterious Musings and Been There, Done That.

Get a Clue • (p. 92)
Use the six clues to figure out the Secret Identity.
Try to guess the answer in as few clues as possible.

Mysterious Musings • (p. 104)
Giving statements "spoken" from the grave, these Secret Identities are all deceased.
The illustrations offer a giant hint to their identities.

Been There, Done That • (p. 118)
Like a connect-the-dots game, the clues in this section are made up of associations that will lead
you to the correct Secret Identity. Each clue deals with a part of the mysterious person's past.

1. I got my start as a futuristic king of the road.

2. I was born in the 1950s.

3. In 2002, I knew what women wanted.

4. I am not related to Cardinals' pitcher Bob Gibson.

5. Danny Glover thought that I was a lethal weapon in the 1990s.

6. In 2004, my film about the death of a biblical figure was one of the top-grossing films of the year.

SOLUTIONS FOUND ON PAGE 222.

92

1. I attended University of Mississippi law school.

2. My career in law led to a stint in my state's legislature.

3. My stories uncover the legal system and the social system in the South.

4. I write about lawyers, guns and money.

5. *Publisher's Weekly* named me the best-selling author of the 1990s.

6. When my books get made into movies, Tom Cruise, Gene Hackman, Julia Roberts and Matt Damon get meaty starring roles.

Get a Clue

1. I am an American athlete.

2. For more than 20 years, I had a ball at work.

3. I am in the Baseball Hall of Fame.

4. My favorite bird is the Oriole.

5. For years, I went to work with my dad and my brother Billy.

6. I surpassed Lou Gehrig's record for consecutive games played.

SOLUTIONS FOUND ON PAGE 222.

93

1. I studied at the University of Maryland.

2. I started my career as a puppeteer.

3. In 1969, I hit the big time on public television with a street full of life-sized puppets.

4. In later life I developed breakthrough television shows like *Fraggle Rock* and *The Storyteller*.

5. If you know my name it is probably because of the street that I built.

6. In the 1970s, my piggish female friend was an international celebrity.

1. I am a living American female.

2. My middle name is Fiona.

3. My brother is also an accomplished actor.

4. I've made nearly as many headlines for my romances with Keifer, Jason and Lyle as I have with my on screen romances with Richard, Dennis and Hugh.

5. My favorite legal expert is Erin Brockovich.

6. I am a Georgia native and an Academy Award®-winning actress.

SOLUTIONS FOUND ON PAGE 222.

1. I am a living American movie director.

2. My controversial film about Christ isn't called *The Passion of the Christ*.

3. Being raised in New York's Little Italy has influenced my movies.

4. In March 2003, I received the Directors Guild of America's Lifetime Achievement Award.

5. Cameron Diaz, Sharon Stone, Paul Newman and Nicolas Cage have all worked for me.

6. My *Taxi Driver* ran into Cybill Shepherd and Jodie Foster.

Get a Clue

1. I made art my day job.

2. I died in 1987.

3. I have my own museum in Pittsburgh, PA.

4. I have no children, but I am called Pop.

5. I did a film satire on Frankenstein.

6. Fifteen minutes became a lifetime for me.

SOLUTIONS FOUND ON PAGE 222.

95

1. I was born in Michigan in 1950 and named Steveland Morris.

2. I lost my eyesight when I was an infant, but I didn't lose my musical abilities.

3. My first big hit was "Fingertips" in 1962.

4. During the 1980s, Paul McCartney and I aired together on MTV, living in perfect harmony.

5. I was inducted into the Rock and Roll Hall of Fame in 1989.

6. I once wrote and sang a tribute to Duke Ellington.

1. I was born in Atlanta, GA.

2. My name sounds like royalty.

3. I married Coretta Scott.

4. I wrote *Why Can't We Wait* in 1964.

5. I preached at Ebenezer Baptist Church.

6. I was named after a key Reformation figure.

SOLUTIONS FOUND ON PAGE 222.

96

1. I share my first name with a planet and a Roman goddess.

2. My sister is a professional tennis player.

3. My balls are usually yellow.

4. I share my last name with a singer named Andy.

5. I was born in 1980.

6. I won at Wimbledon in 2000.

Get a Clue

1. My "Revolution" was not set in Russia.

2. I am nude on an album cover.

3. My mates started as metallic bugs.

4. My son Sean and I were born on the same day of the same month.

5. My first band was The Quarrymen.

6. I'm half of one of the most famous song-writing teams of all time.

SOLUTIONS FOUND ON PAGE 222.

97

1. I am a living American male.

2. I grew up in Oakland, CA.

3. I'm not a weight lifter, but I won an award for being big.

4. People started talking about me when I fell in love with a mermaid.

5. In my early career, having *Bosom Buddies* was essential.

6. My wife is actress Rita Wilson.

1. I was born in 1963 in Brooklyn, New York.

2. I attended the University of North Carolina.

3. I worked part-time for a shoe company for nearly 20 years.

4. Although I'm not a pilot, my nickname is "Air."

5. No bull, I am best known as a professional athlete.

6. For three years, people called me a Wizard.

SOLUTIONS FOUND ON PAGE 222.

98

1. I was born in Fairfield, CT in 1961.

2. My friends knew me as Margaret Mary Emily Ann Hyra when I was a kid.

3. Walter Matthau played my uncle, Albert Einstein, in a movie.

4. In real life, Dennis Quaid and I lived in San Francisco's Pacific Heights in a house that Kent McCarthy bought.

5. I proved to Harry that women can easily fake orgasms.

6. In the movies, I've played Lt. Goose's wife, Jim Morrison's girlfriend and the long distance love interest of Jonah's dad.

GEt a Clue

1. I was born in Brooklyn, NY in 1935.

2. I am a neurotic, clarinet playing, writer/director/actor.

3. My parents are Mr. and Mrs. Konigsberg.

4. My first screenplay was *What's New, Pussycat?*

5. Diane Keaton worked for me a lot during the 1970s.

6. I've spent the last thirty years exploring my mind's idea of how people relate through a series of films that sometimes work and sometimes don't but I don't care, because the important thing to me is to get these stories and characters out of my head. Oh God, here I go again… It's crazy. Help me.

SOLUTIONS FOUND ON PAGE 222.

99

1. I was born in Minnesota in 1921 and was called Frances as a child.

2. I got my start at the Chicago World's Fair in 1933 as one of the Gumm Sisters.

3. I was friends with the Rat Pack.

4. I had five husbands, but was never married to Mickey Rooney.

5. My daughters are Liza and Lorna.

6. I sang "(Dear Mr. Gable) You Made Me Love You" to Clark on his 36th birthday.

1. I grew up in the 1930s in orphanages and foster homes.

2. Though I was married to a great athlete and a famous playwright, I'm best known as a movie actress.

3. Billy Joel mentions me in his song, "We Didn't Start The Fire."

4. I'm no doctor, but I tried to cure an itch.

5. I don't know if you know my name, but JFK sure did after I sang to him on his birthday.

6. I was in the first issue of *Playboy*.

SOLUTIONS FOUND ON PAGE 222.

100

1. I was born in Santa Monica, CA in 1928.

2. I am an American female.

3. A popular drink was named after me.

4. I helped introduce Mr. Bojangles decades before Jerry Jeff Walker's song.

5. During the 1970s I served as Ambassador to Ghana.

6. My married last name is a color.

Get a Clue

1. I am best known for my work in the movies.

2. If you've seen *Deliverance*, you've seen my Pop on the river.

3. I helped bring Lara Croft from cyberspace to the silver screen.

4. I won an Academy Award® for playing a sociopathic inmate in a psychiatric hospital.

5. You shouldn't be surprised to find me in a tattoo parlor.

6. My Billy and my Bob were the same person.

SOLUTIONS FOUND ON PAGE 222.

101

1. I spent a good deal of my adult life in a wheelchair.

2. I married my second cousin.

3. The US Constitution was changed after my death.

4. I'm not Monty Hall, but I love to offer New Deals.

5. If Hoover is known for the Great Depression, I'm known for World War II.

6. I was the governor of New York before becoming President of the US.

Armchair Puzzlers • Secret Identities

1. I am best known as an author.

2. I created Gerald McBoing-Boing.

3. I like to rhyme, but I'm no Longfellow.

4. My film *Hitler Lives* won an Oscar® for best documentary.

5. In 1937, I went to Mulberry Street and saw some cool stuff.

6. I invented the term "nerd."

SOLUTIONS FOUND ON PAGE 222.

1. I am best known as a rock musician.

2. I'm no Romeo but I surround myself with heartbreakers.

3. I lent my voice to an episode of *The Simpsons*.

4. My name suggests that I might make a big deal out of nothing.

5. I know an "American Girl" when I see one.

6. In the 1980s, I was a Traveling Wilbury.

GEt a CLUe

1. I am a soulful singer.

2. I appeared on Motown's Tamla label in the 1960s.

3. In 1987, I was the first woman to be inducted into the Rock and Roll Hall of Fame.

4. I appeared in *The Blues Brothers* with Dan Aykroyd and John Belushi.

5. I sang at the inauguration of President Bill Clinton and at the wedding of Vice President Al Gore's daughter, Karenna.

6. Respect is really important to me.

103

SOLUTIONS FOUND ON PAGE 222.

1. I was born in the late 1970s, and that decade has done wonders for my career.

2. I've modeled for Versace and Calvin Klein.

3. I am known for losing my car, dude.

4. My friends are glad that I've decided to stop punking them.

5. Though I don't use it, my first name is Christopher.

6. Demi Moore knows that my favorite months are May and December.

Mysterious Musings

SOLUTIONS FOUND ON PAGE 222.

104

"Hi. I was born in Florida, MO in 1835. My mother called me Sam and was surprised when I became a steamship captain on the Mississippi River. I had a series of interesting jobs, including a stint in the Confederate Army during the Civil War, before I found my calling as a humorist. During my 50-year career I wrote about many topics, including frogs in California, King Arthur and a couple of boys growing up in Missouri." Do you know my pen name?

Mysterious musings

"I was born the son of a glove maker and a farm girl in Stratford-upon-Avon during the 16th century. I was an actor during my early years and discovered my love for watching, directing and writing plays. My life's work has lasted the test of time and I am considered the most read author on the planet, as well as one of the most quoted."
Dost thou knowest my name?

SOLUTIONS FOUND ON PAGE 222.

105

SOLUTIONS FOUND ON PAGE 222.

106

"I am known as a man of peace and as a force of change. I did a great deal of my work in a poor Asian country that was under British rule. I don't eat meat and didn't actually eat much at all while making a name for myself. My life's goal was achieved in 1947."

Who am I?

Mysterious musings

SOLUTIONS FOUND ON PAGE 222.

"When I was born in England in 1820, it wasn't much of an event. But during the Crimean War, I made a name for myself. Now I encourage women to contribute to helping the needy. I was a pioneer for social change and I founded a school for midwives and nurses."

Whatzmyname?

Armchair Puzzlers • Secret Identities

Mysterious Musings

SOLUTIONS FOUND ON PAGE 222.

108

"Buon giorno! I was born in Italy in the 15th century, but accomplished more on the other side of the Atlantic Ocean. My claim to fame came when the Queen of Spain paid me to take three ladies on a long sailing trip to a faraway land."

Whatzmyname?

Mysterious Musings

"I love to be in the air, just like John Glenn loved it 30 years after me. I am most famous for my trip to Paris, but fame has not always been my friend. The kidnapping of my son in 1932 was a tragic event that put me back in the world news. I lived in Connecticut and England and I died in Hawaii."

Whatzmyname?

SOLUTIONS FOUND ON PAGE 222.

109

Mysterious musings

SOLUTIONS FOUND ON PAGE 222.

110

"I am a Brit who left home at 14 and joined the circus. I learned how to do comedy and became a professional stilt walker. In the 1930s, I made a name for myself in the movies and once played C.K. Dexter Haven to Katharine Hepburn's Tracy Lord. In the 1940s and 1950s I starred in several Alfred Hitchcock films. Although I am known as a man of grace and charm, I ended up dying in 1986 in the farming community of Davenport, IA." My real initials are A.L. but what name do you know me by?

Mysterious musings

"I had a short, volatile life before my death in 1945, but my single literary effort regarding life during World War II has left a lasting impression on the western world. Movies have been made about the time I spent in Holland. My darkest secrets, including my crush on Peter van Daan, have been exposed."

Whatzmyname?

SOLUTIONS FOUND ON PAGE 222.

Mysterious Musings

SOLUTIONS FOUND ON PAGE 222.

112

"I never thought my short trip with William Dawes back in the 18th century would impress people enough to have a Massachusetts city named after me, but it did. I went from being a master engraver to the subject of songs and even a Longfellow poem. Ironically, all of the credit should go to my horse, Brown Beauty, who made the dark midnight ride possible."

Giddyup and guess my name.

Mysterious Musings

"I would have been famous in history even without Shakespeare's plays and Cecil B. DeMille's epic 1934 film about me. Known only by my first name, I was a queen in Roman times. I love men and even married my brothers. Although I traveled the Nile River, many have said that I lived my life as if it was a river of denial."

I command you to announce my name.

SOLUTIONS FOUND ON PAGE 222.

Mysterious Musings

"I was born a subject of the British Empire, but after reading John Locke and Jean-Jacques Rousseau, I decided that man had certain inalienable rights that could not be taken away or denied. I owned a big farm in Virginia and was more interested in architecture and investments than politics. I really admired the French and spent several years in Paris as the American minister to France. I died on the 4th of July, on the same day as my old adversary John Adams."

Whatzmyname?

SOLUTIONS FOUND ON PAGE 222.

114

Mysterious mUsings

"I was born Elisabeth Griscom in 1752. I opened an upholstery shop with my husband in Philadelphia on Arch Street and quickly became an expert seamstress. I was married three times, but my biggest accomplishment was the design and creation of my nation's most important symbol."

Whatzmyname?

SOLUTIONS FOUND ON PAGE 222.

Mysterious musings

"I have an amazing lineage with a mortal mother and the god Zeus as my father. You probably have heard that I am considered the most beautiful woman on Earth and that a decade-long war was fought in ancient Greece to get me back home. Once returned to my people, I married Menelaus, despite my love for another man."

Whatzmyname?

SOLUTIONS FOUND ON PAGE 222.

116

Armchair Puzzlers • Secret Identities

Mysterious m*usings*

"I was born in 1412 in a small French village. Although I was not a great political or business leader, I did have a "strong vision" about the direction my people should take. I worked with Charles VII to help him defeat the English and begin his reign as king. My story might have ended there if not for my capture and conviction of heresy by the church. Despite my later canonization, in 1431 I was burned at the stake in Rouen as a relapsed heretic."

Whatzmyname?

SOLUTIONS FOUND ON PAGE 222.

BEEN THERE > < DONE THAT

1. *Paint Your Wagon*

2. Climbed the Eiger

3. Co-starred with Clyde (the orangutan)

4. Sondra Locke

1. *Guys and Dolls*

2. Paul Whiteman

3. "Chairman of the Board"

4. Hoboken, NJ

SOLUTIONS FOUND ON PAGE 223.

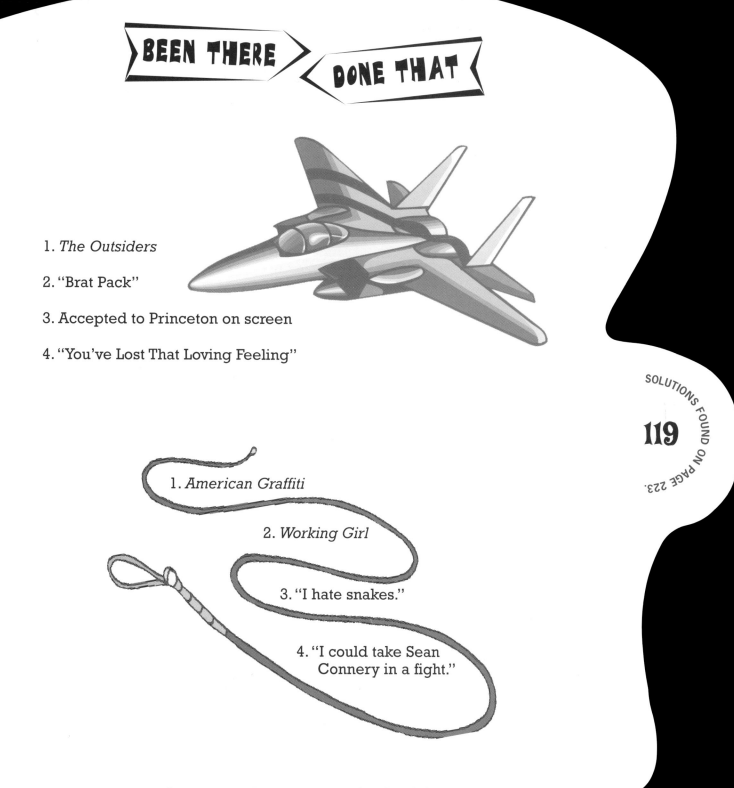

BEEN THERE > < DONE THAT

1. *The Outsiders*

2. "Brat Pack"

3. Accepted to Princeton on screen

4. "You've Lost That Loving Feeling"

1. *American Graffiti*

2. *Working Girl*

3. "I hate snakes."

4. "I could take Sean Connery in a fight."

SOLUTIONS FOUND ON PAGE 223.

119

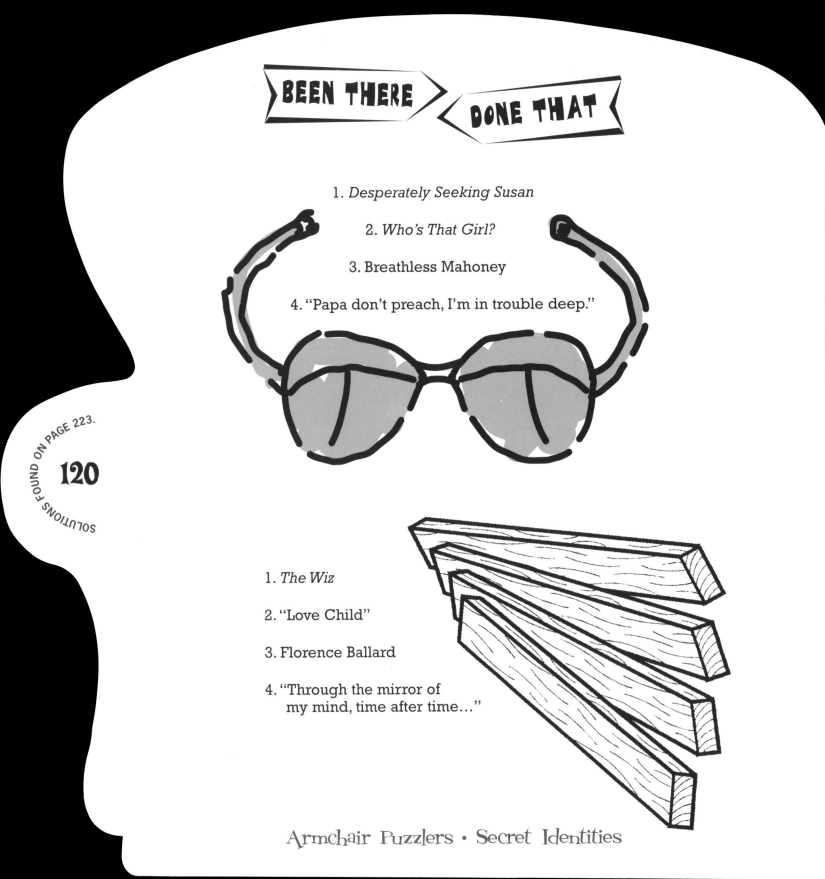

BEEN THERE DONE THAT

1. *Desperately Seeking Susan*

2. *Who's That Girl?*

3. Breathless Mahoney

4. "Papa don't preach, I'm in trouble deep."

1. *The Wiz*

2. "Love Child"

3. Florence Ballard

4. "Through the mirror of my mind, time after time…"

SOLUTIONS FOUND ON PAGE 223.

120

Armchair Puzzlers • Secret Identities

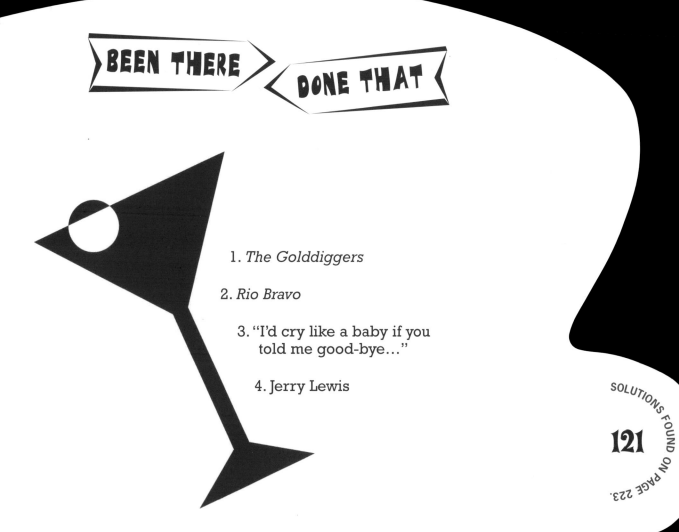

BEEN THERE > < DONE THAT

1. *The Golddiggers*

2. *Rio Bravo*

3. "I'd cry like a baby if you told me good-bye…"

4. Jerry Lewis

SOLUTIONS FOUND ON PAGE 223.

121

1. *Rebel Without a Cause*

2. Appeared in old TV Westerns

3. *Hoosiers*

4. "We did it, man. We did it, we did it. We're rich, man. We're retirin' in Florida now, mister."

Armchair Puzzlers · Secret Identities

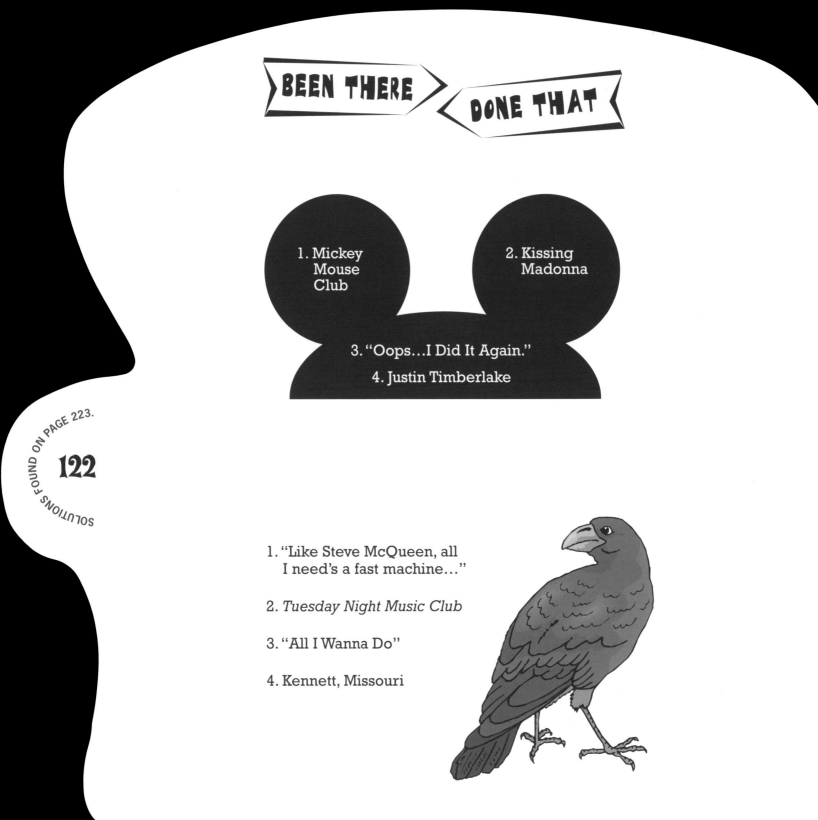

BEEN THERE > DONE THAT

1. Mickey Mouse Club

2. Kissing Madonna

3. "Oops...I Did It Again."

4. Justin Timberlake

SOLUTIONS FOUND ON PAGE 223.

122

1. "Like Steve McQueen, all I need's a fast machine..."

2. *Tuesday Night Music Club*

3. "All I Wanna Do"

4. Kennett, Missouri

BEEN THERE DONE THAT

1. Loyal soldier in Boer War

2. Yalta Conference with Roosevelt and Stalin

3. "The Iron Curtain"

4. Cigar smoker

SOLUTIONS FOUND ON PAGE 223.

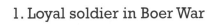

1. Famous film director

2. *Psycho* and *Family Plot*

3. "Good evening."

4. "Funeral March of a Marionette"

Armchair Puzzlers · Secret Identities

BEEN THERE **DONE THAT**

1. "You're fired!"

2. Taj Mahal

3. Real estate mogul

4. Ivana

SOLUTIONS FOUND ON PAGE 223.

124

1. Margaritas

2. *A Pirate Looks at Fifty*

3. "The weather is here, I wish you were beautiful."

4. The Coral Reefers

1. "Heeeere's Johnny!"

2. *Easy Rider*

3. Angelica Huston

4. Randle Patrick McMurphy

SOLUTIONS FOUND ON PAGE 223.

125

1. "Danger Prone" Daphne Blake

2. *All My Children*

3. Freddie Prinze Jr.

4. *I Know What You Did Last Summer*

BEEN THERE DONE THAT

TAXI

1. TriBeCa Films

2. "You talkin' to me? You talkin' to me?"

3. Jake LaMotta

4. The Mafia

SOLUTIONS FOUND ON PAGE 223.

1. "Got a wife and kids in Baltimore, Jack…"

2. Asbury Park

3. "The Boss"

4. Nebraska

Armchair Puzzlers • Secret Identities

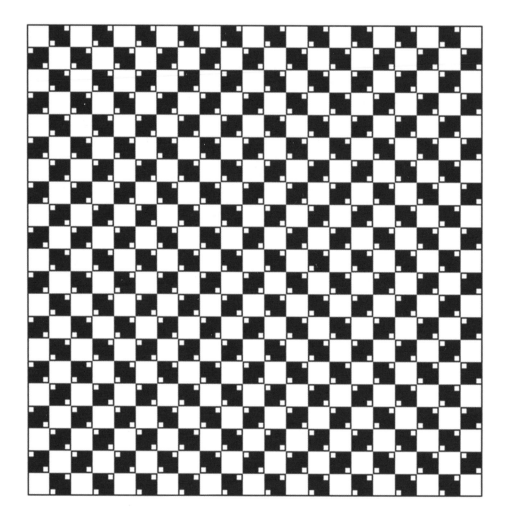

KITAOKA'S WAVES
Do the lines appear to be wavy?

Answer: They are all perfectly straight.

Armchair Puzzlers • Optical Teasers

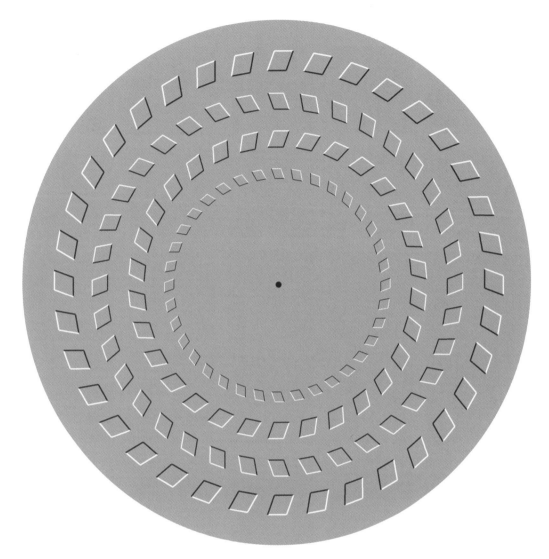

THE REVOLVING CIRCLES ILLUSION

Move your head slowly toward and away from the image and you will see something very strange! The circles will turn in different ways.

THE HERMANN GRID ILLUSION
Count the faint dark dots at the intersections.
When you are done, try counting again.
If you stare at any one dot, it will disappear.

Armchair Puzzlers • Optical Teasers

THE OUCHI ILLUSION

Slowly shake this image. The center section will
appear to separate from the rest of the image.

132

TWISTED CIRCLES

Do you see a series of warped circles? Try tracing
the lines. Be careful! It is really a series of
circles, each one within a larger circle.

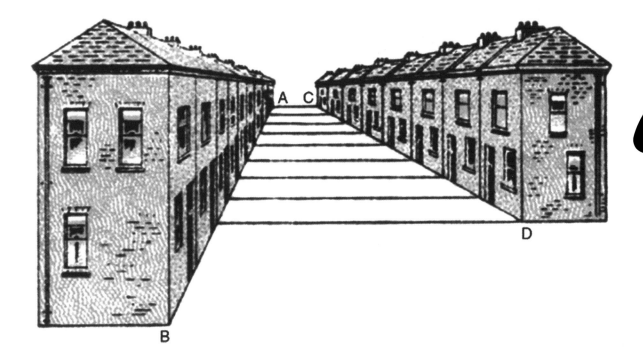

133

AN ILLUSION OF EXTENT
Which line is longer: Line A-B or Line C-D?

Answer: They are both the same length.

Armchair Puzzlers • Optical Teasers

134

X91086

A SURPRISED POLICEMAN
This policeman will look really surprised
when you turn him upside down.

SCHOOL OF FISH
Are the fish swimming to the right or to the left?

Answer: Both! If you stare at the image, they will appear to reverse direction.

Armchair Puzzlers • Optical Teasers

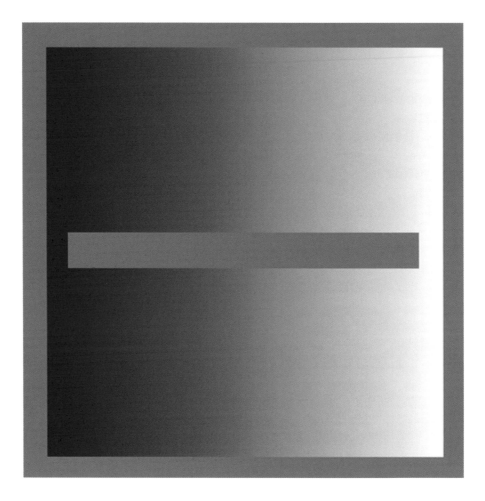

SIMULTANEOUS CONTRAST ILLUSION
Is the horizontal bar lighter on the left and darker on the right? Try covering everything surrounding the bar to check your answer.

Answer: The bar is the same color on both sides.

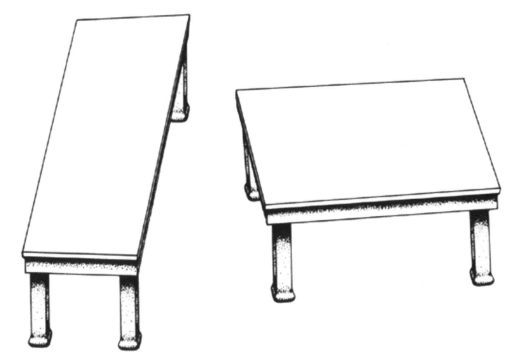

SHEPARD'S TABLETOP ILLUSION
Which tabletop appears larger?
Carefully measure them to check your answer.

Answer: They are both equal.

Armchair Puzzlers • Optical Teasers

138

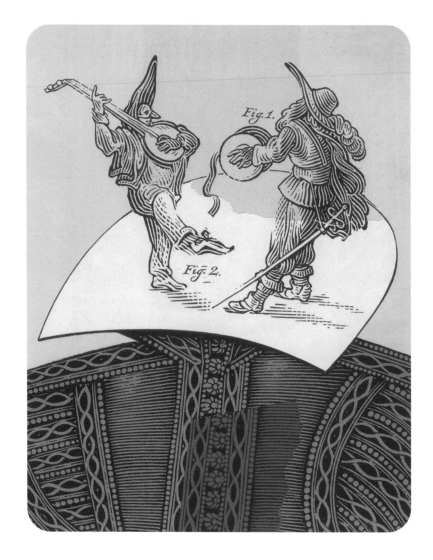

ALL THE WORLD'S A STAGE

Two musicians gather together to form the face of
the famous 16th century English playwright
William Shakespeare.

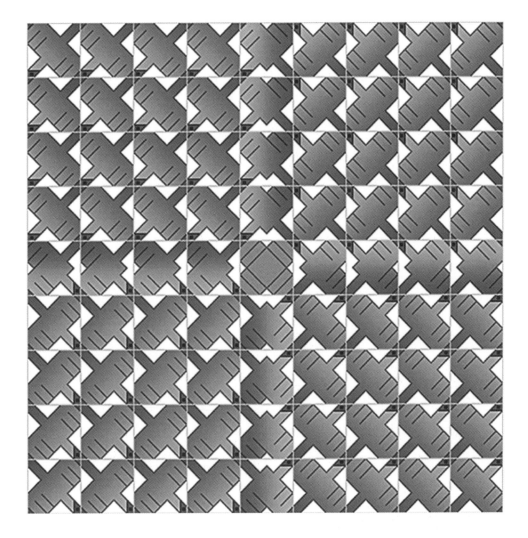

THE CAFÉ ESCHER ILLUSION
Do the horizontal and vertical lines bend?
Check them with a straight edge.

Answer: The lines are perfectly straight.

Armchair Puzzlers • Optical Teasers

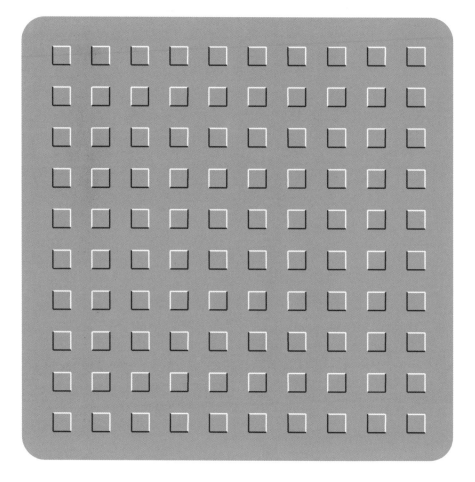

PINNA'S DEFORMING SQUARE ILLUSION
Try slowly shaking and turning this image.
The squares will appear to change shape and wiggle.

141

MY WIFE AND MOTHER-IN-LAW
Try to find both an old and young woman.

Answer: The eye of the old woman becomes the ear of the young woman. The mouth of the old woman becomes a necklace on the young woman.

142

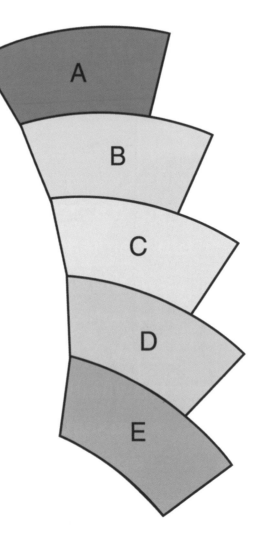

THE WUNDT ILLUSION
E appears larger than D, which appears larger than C,
which appears larger than B, which appears larger than A.
So, which is the largest shape?

Answer: They are all equal in size and shape.

Armchair Puzzlers • Optical Teasers

143

THE IMPOSSIBLE FORK

Do you see two rectangular prongs
or three cylindrical prongs?

144

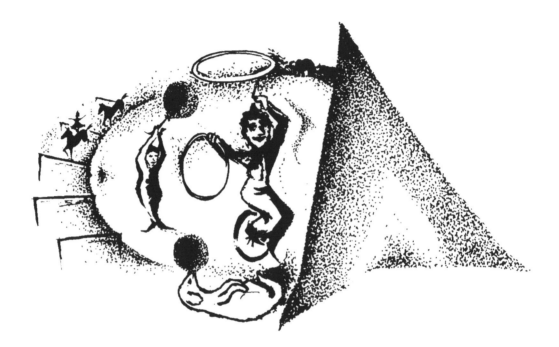

THE MISSING CLOWN
The circus seems to have lost its clown.
Try to find him.

KITCHEN UTENSILS
How many kitchen utensils can you find?

145

Answer: Don't forget to count both the black and white kitchen utensils.

146

THE CAPTAIN HAS ABANDONED SHIP
During the storm, the ship seems to have lost its captain. Try to find him.

Answer: Turn the image 90° clockwise to find him.

DOES HE SPEAK THE TRUTH?
Is this man telling the truth?
The answer is written in his face.

Answer: He is a liar. Turn the image 90° counterclockwise to see why.

147

THE SCINTILLATING GRID ILLUSION
Count the faint dark dots at the intersections.
When you are done, try counting again.
If you stare at any one dot, it will disappear.

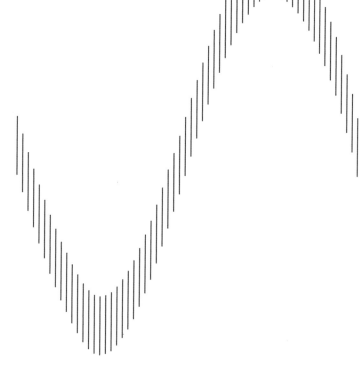

DAY'S SINE WAVE ILLUSION
Are some vertical lines longer than others in this wave pattern?

Answer: They are all of equal length.

Armchair Puzzlers • Optical Teasers

150

CAN A FROG TURN INTO A HORSE?
This strange frog won't turn into a prince. But it will turn into a horse! Can you figure out how?

Answer: Turn the image 90° counterclockwise to find the horse.

ESTIMATION ILLUSION
How far up the triangle is the dot?

Answer: It is exactly in the middle.

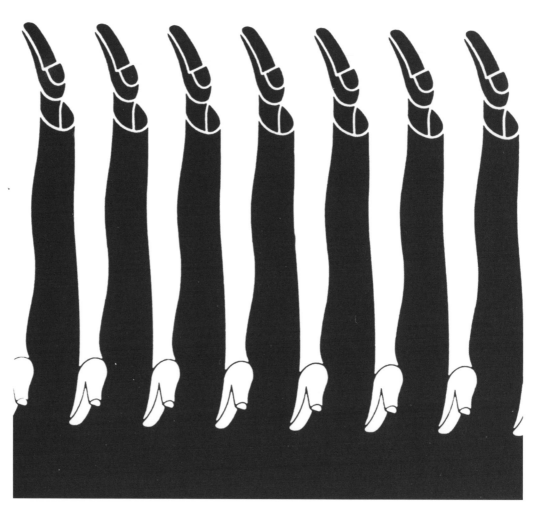

LEGS OF TWO DIFFERENT GENDERS
Can you see both the women's and men's legs?

KITAOKA'S SPA ILLUSION

Move the image up and down slowly, and you will
see the little shapes moving in strange ways.

MORELLET'S TIRET ILLUSION
Move your eyes around the edge of this
image and it will appear to flash.

ASSIMILATION ILLUSION
Is the gray square in the middle darker than the surrounding gray?

Answer: They are equal shades of gray.

Armchair Puzzlers • Optical Teasers

155

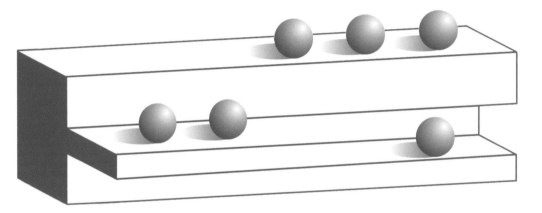

THE IMPOSSIBLE SHELF
What is wrong with this shelf?

THE HERING ILLUSION
Do the long lines bend?

Answer : They are all straight.

TERRA SUBTERRANEA

Is the monster in the background larger
than the monster in the front?
Try measuring each figure to test your answer.

Answer: They are equal in size.

THE MYSTERIOUS LIPS
Can you find the woman's face?

Answer: The houses are the eyes.

159

Armchair Puzzlers • Optical Teasers

160

WHERE IS THE DOG'S MASTER?
This dog has lost its master. Try to find him.

REFLECT ON THIS

These numbers do not seem to add up correctly.
Is there any way that you can make them add up correctly?
You may have to reflect on this one a while.

Answer: Look at this image in a mirror.

Armchair Puzzlers • Optical Teasers

COMING AND GOING
How can you make the ducks change direction?

Answer: Cover either the left or right outermost head.

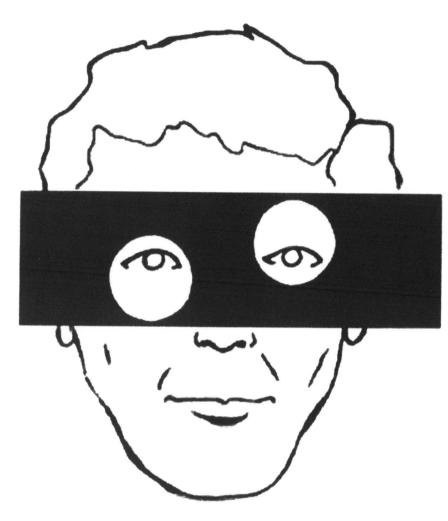

MISALIGNED EYES
Does this man have crooked eyes?
Check them with a straight edge.

Answer: His eyes are perfectly aligned.

Armchair Puzzlers • Optical Teasers

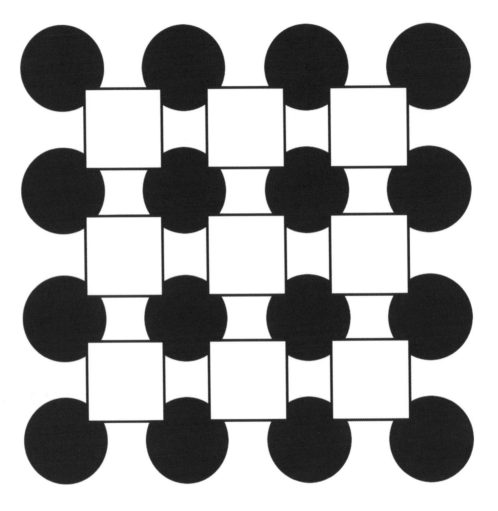

MOCHI
Are the squares bent?

Answer: All the squares have straight edges.

Armchair Puzzlers • Optical Teasers

LET SLEEPING DOGS LIE

People on this island have an expression:
"Let sleeping dogs lie." Why do you think that is?

Answer: The island is two sleeping dogs.

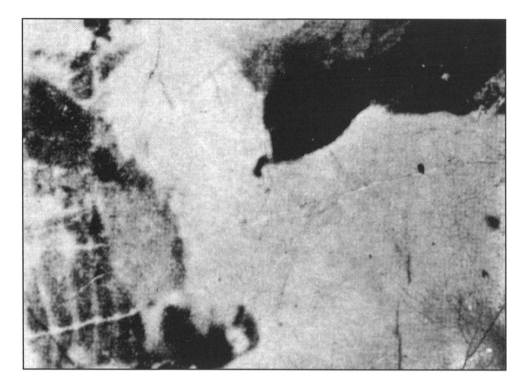

FIGURE/GROUND ILLUSION #1
What does this image represent?

Answer: The head of a cow.

Armchair Puzzlers • Optical Teasers

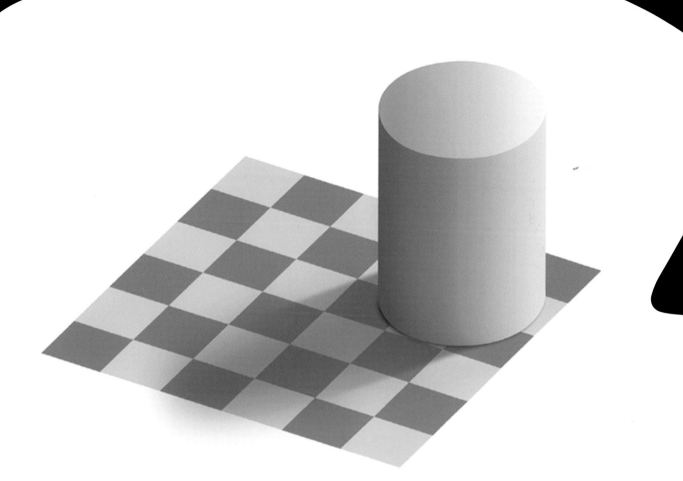

ADELSON'S CHECKER-SHADOW ILLUSION

Are the light squares within the shadow the same shade of gray as the dark squares outside the shadow? Look through a small peephole to check.

Answer: They are the same shade of gray.

168

THE GLOWING LIGHTBULB
Stare at this lightbulb for 30 seconds
or more without averting your gaze.
Quickly look at a blank sheet of paper
and you will see a glowing lightbulb.

WHISTLER REX

169

WHERE IS THE QUEEN?
The king appears to have lost his queen.
Find her and put your finger on her hair.

Answer: Turn the king upside down.

Armchair Puzzlers • Optical Teasers

KISSING COUPLE
Do you see one head or two
heads kissing?

RUBIN'S FACE/VASE ILLUSION
Can you find the two profiles?

Answer: They are on either side of the vase.

Armchair Puzzlers • Optical Teasers

172

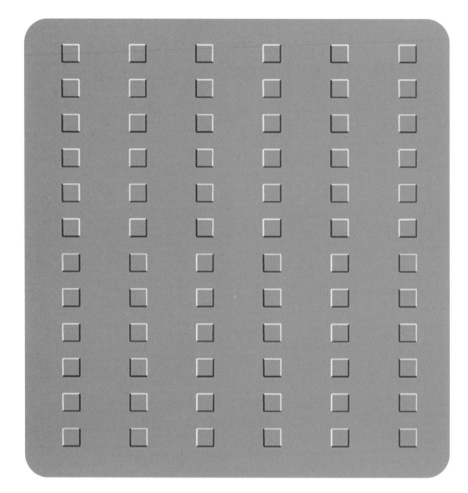

SPLITTING LINES ILLUSION
Slowly move the image up and down
and the lines will split.

Armchair Puzzlers • Optical Teasers

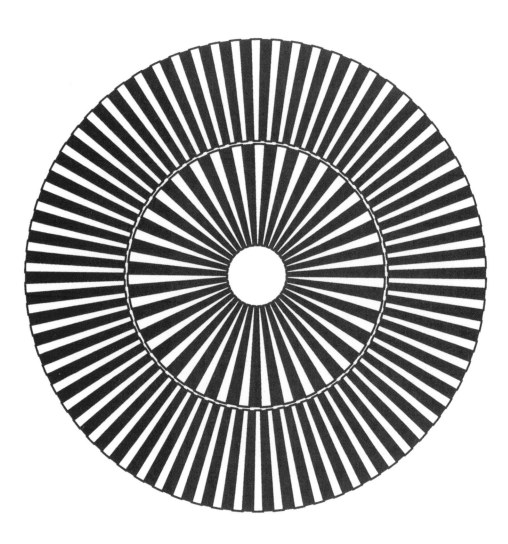

THE HULA HOOP ILLUSION
Slowly move this image in a circular fashion,
like you are swirling water in a cup.

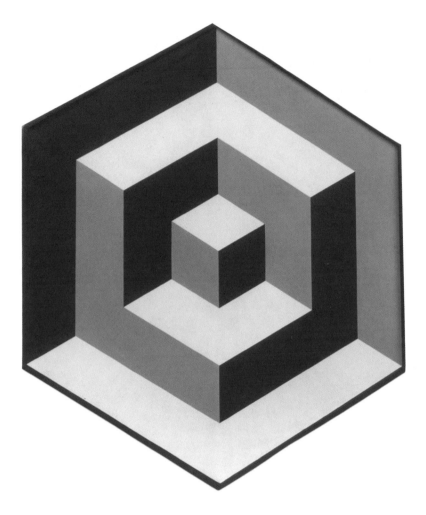

REVERSIBLE CUBE
If you stare at this image long enough, it will reverse.
The insides of the cubes will become
the outsides of the cubes.

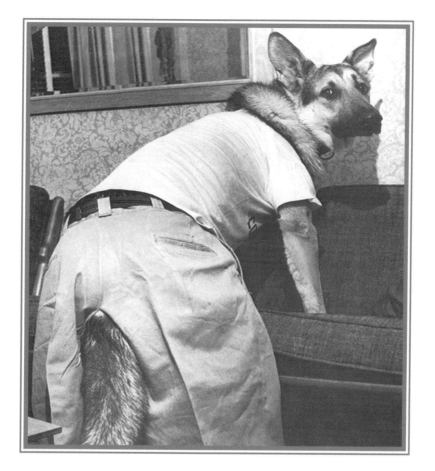

A DOG'S LIFE
Does this dog think it is human?

HELEN KELLER
This portrait of Helen Keller, who was blind
since birth, is made entirely out of Braille.

176

EGYPTIAN TÊTE-À-TÊTE
Do you see one face or two faces?

Answer: There is one face behind the candlestick and two on each side of the candlestick.

Armchair Puzzlers • Optical Teasers

FIGURE/GROUND ILLUSION #2
What does this image represent?

Answer: A Dalmatian dog.

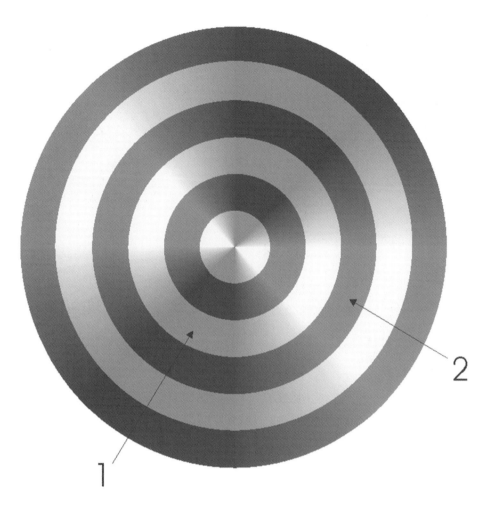

TODOROVIC'S DARTBOARD ILLUSION
Is the light area at position 1 lighter than the dark area at position 2?

Answer: Believe it or not, they are identical.

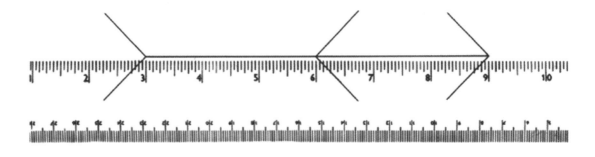

MULLER-LYER ILLUSION
Which horizontal length between the arrows is longer? Does the ruler help?

Answer: The lengths are equal.

Armchair Puzzlers • Optical Teasers

THE TWISTED CORD ILLUSION
Do the vertical lines bend?

Answer: They are perfectly straight.

181

182

UPSIDE DOWN

UPSIDE DOWN

What does this say when you
turn it upside down?

183

L'EGISTENTIAL QUANDRY
Why might this elephant have some
difficulty walking?

184

REFLECTIONS ON THE WORD MIRROR
You can read the word mirror front to back.

185

TILT INDUCTION ILLUSION
Do the two vertical lines tilt away from each other?

Answer: They are parallel to each other.

Armchair Puzzlers • Optical Teasers

EHRENSTEIN ILLUSION

Do you see circles, even though there are no edges to make them? Do they appear to be brighter than their surroundings?

Answer: The circles are illusory and so is their brightness.

Armchair Puzzlers • Optical Teasers

187

FISHEYE ILLUSION
Move this image close to your eye.
It will no longer appear distorted.

KITAOKA'S KOZOLL
Do the horizontal lines tilt with respect to each other?

Answer: They are all parallel to each other.

A MOUSE HIDING FROM A CAT
This mouse is pretty clever!
Can you find where it is hiding from the cat?

190

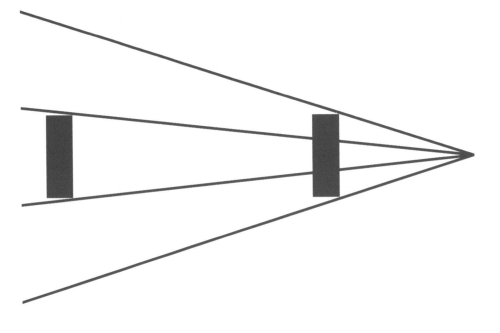

THE PONZO ILLUSION
Is the bar on the left smaller than the bar on the right?

Answer: They are equal in size.

Armchair Puzzlers • Optical Teasers

191

TIME-SAVING SUGGESTION
Try to see both the running figures and the arrows.

ILLUSORY SPOTS AND CIRCLES
Do you see a series of concentric rings
made of little dots?

Answer: Both the dots and the rings are illusory.

A BOY GROWS A BEARD
Can you help this boy turn into a man?

193

Answer: Turn him upside down and he will grow a beard.

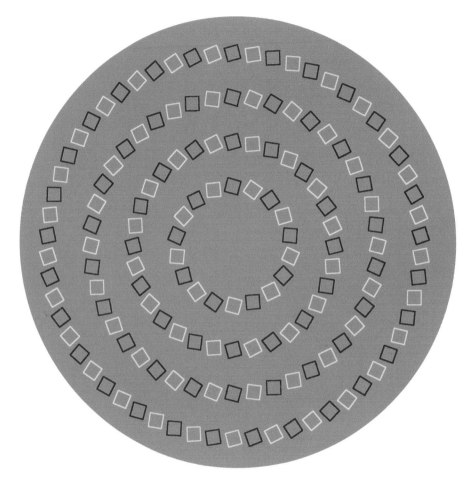

PINNA'S INTERTWINING ILLUSION
Do these rings cross over each other?

Answer: They do not cross over each other. They are concentric circles.

194

EYE AM A MOUTH

The eyes become the mouths.

Armchair Puzzlers • Optical Teasers

196

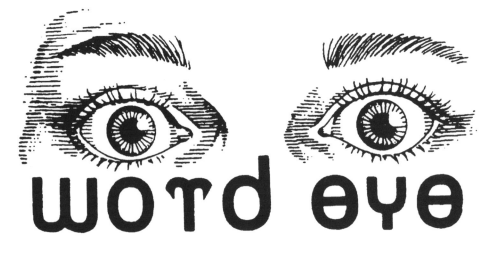

word eye

BACKWARDS GLANCE
What does this say when you read it in a mirror?

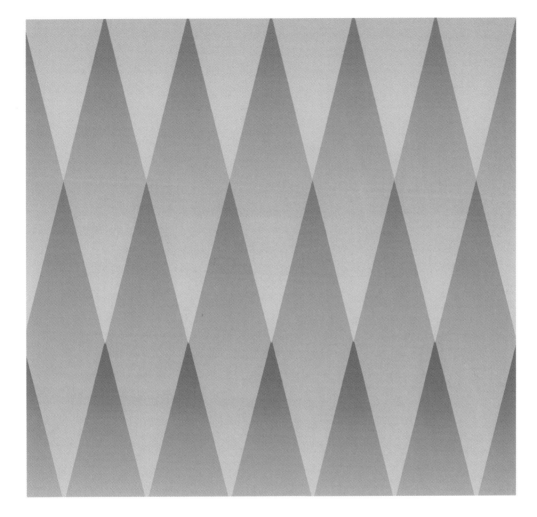

DIAMOND BRIGHTNESS ILLUSION
Is the row of triangles on the bottom darker than the row at the top?

Answer: They are identical shades of gray.

Armchair Puzzlers • Optical Teasers

198

SAILING THROUGH THE PALM TREES
Try to see both the palm trees and the boats.

AN ARTIST'S VIEW OF REALITY
What is strange about this painting?

Armchair Puzzlers • Optical Teasers

200

TWO BODIES ARE BETTER THAN ONE
In this unretouched photograph, does the head
belong to the lady on the left or on the right?

Answer: Left

201

RISING LINES

Hold the page at eye level and look across it from the bottom right corner. The lines will appear to rise from the page.

202

SARA NADER
Can you see the woman the musician is serenading?

THE HALLWAY ILLUSION
Does the man on the far right seem tiny compared
with the man in the background? Measure them.

Answer: They are the same size.

Armchair Puzzlers • Optical Teasers

203

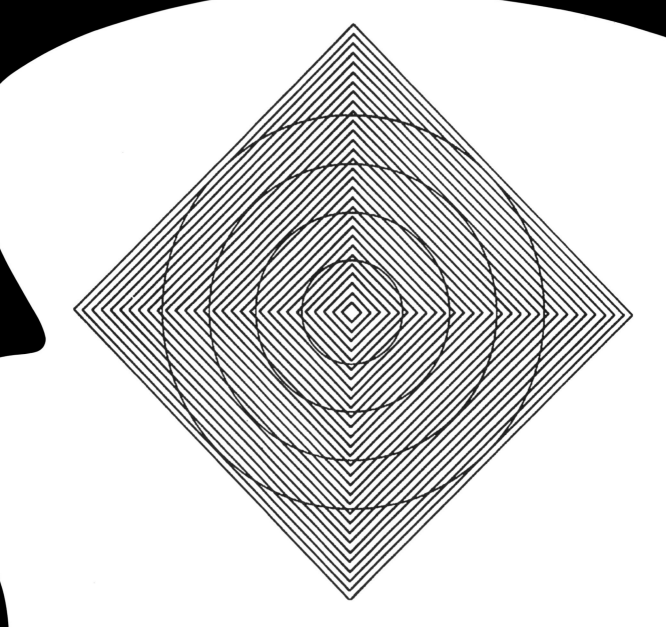

BENT CIRCLES
Do the circles bend?

Answer: They are perfectly round.

204

205

A GLOWING PORTRAIT

Stare at this image for at least 30 seconds without moving your eyes and then quickly look at a blank sheet of paper. You will see the woman appear to glow.

206

WADE'S SPIRAL

Do you perceive a spiral?
Carefully trace it with your finger.

Answer: It is a series of concentric circles.

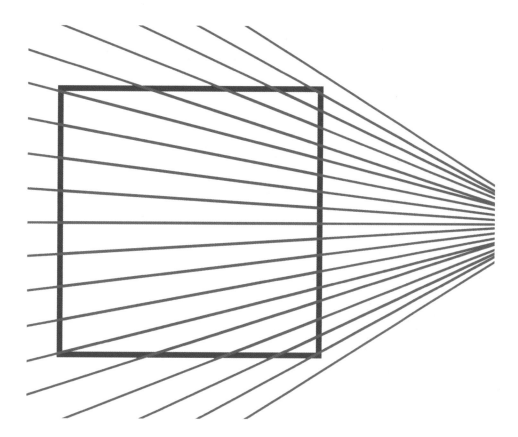

DISTORTED SQUARE ILLUSION
Is the left side of the square shorter than the right side?

Answer: They are the same length.

Armchair Puzzlers • Optical Teasers

207

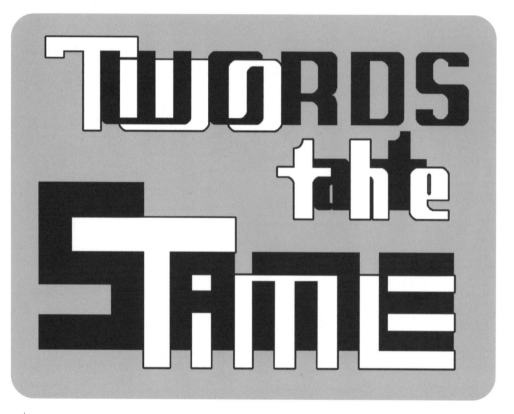

A SPEED READING TEST
Read all the words simultaneously.
What do they say?

Answer: Two words at the same time.

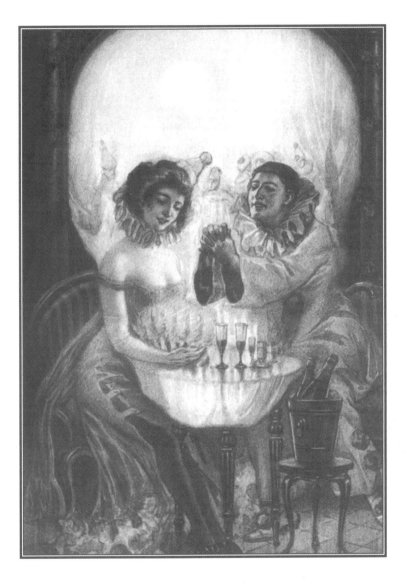

209

A SENSE OF FOREBODING
Is there danger lurking for this couple?

Answer: There is a skull in the background.

210

GLEE TURNS GLUM
You can change the mood of these faces
by turning them upside down.

211

JASTROW'S DUCK/RABBIT ILLUSION
Try to find both the duck and the rabbit.

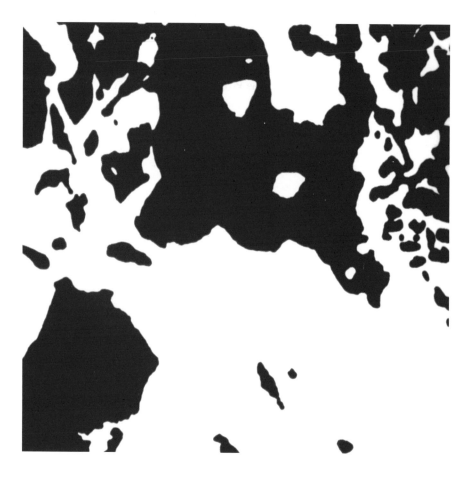

WHAT'S THIS?
What does this image represent?

Answer: A bearded man

213

IMPOSSIBLE FIGURES
Examine all of these figures.
What is strange about them?

Answer: They are all impossible.

Armchair Puzzlers • Optical Teasers

the end

THE END IS IN SIGHT
Why was this illusion placed at the very end?
Turn it upside down to find out.

Answer: The End

Armchair Puzzlers · Optical Teasers

Puzzle Solutions

215

Brainteasers

Page 6
Precedent or President
An economist. Peter thinks of US dollars when he thinks of these presidents.

Washington = $1
Lincoln = $5
Jackson = $20

Page 6
Alphabet Soup
e, t, a: tea (beverage), eat (verb), ate (homonym)

Page 7
The Circle Game
A square has a larger area, since the circle with a 1-foot diameter will actually fit inside a square with a 1-foot side.

Page 7
Paw-Paws Handyman
2 hours (Emmitt can paint 1/3 of the room in an hour while Quincy can paint 1/6 of the room in an hour. In 2 hours they will paint 2/3 + 2/6 = 1 entire painted room.)

Page 8
Panhandling
Alaska, Michigan, Oklahoma, Texas, West Virginia

Page 8
Pied Piper Wanted
4 rats: There are only 4 corners to the room.

Page 9
The Disappearing Pickle
Three. If he sold half of his pickles, that would leave him with one and a half. Then selling a half, he has one pickle left.

Page 9
Blue Light Special
House numbers

Page 10
Lost in Space
State of confusion! More likely close to Burlington, Iowa.

Page 10
Over Easy
Humpty Dumpty

Page 11
Stand and Sign
William H. Taft started the tradition of the 7th inning stretch. He also is the only man to become Chief Justice of the Supreme Court after his presidency (1909-1913).

Page 11
Wordly Wise
Without a period after the word "vehicles," the sign clearly told Alva that his car would not be towed. Mr. Smith, a high school English teacher, cleared up the grammar issues for the judge. Alva had a good case and won in traffic court.

Page 12
Food, Please
The tin can (This allowed armies to travel longer distances without having to search for farmers who could feed them. Fresh food spoiled after a few days, but the new canned rations kept Napoleon's army marching for weeks at a time.)

Page 12
Winter Construction
Cold water (She wouldn't feel how hot the hot water was and could burn herself badly.)

Page 13
Most Wanted
Jeff   (Jefferson City, MO)
Harris   (Harrisburg, PA)
Sal   (Salem, OR)
Al   (Albany, NY)

Page 13
No Blankety Blanks
A. Meg stopped the asp with a quick stab of the spear that she held with her right hand.
B. The man was really tired since the wheel weighed a ton.

Page 14
Light Show
A kaleidoscope

Page 14
Color Blind
Major League Baseball umpire's underwear (black)
A Catholic novice's garb (white)
Archie Andrew's hair (red)
Stitching on a baseball (red)
Wimbledon tennis players' dress code (white)

Page 15
Family Matters
False. If he has a widow, he is dead.

Page 15
Dog Dayz
J (June-the letters are the first letter of the months of the year in reverse order.)

Brainteasers

Page 16
Just Kidding
The third kid was a baby goat.

Page 16
Buried Treasure
Yes (It is illegal to bury a living person.)

Page 17
Go West, Young Woman
1:00 pm (There is a three-hour time difference.)

Page 17
I am Counting on You
One thousand (ten hundred) and two, 1002.

Page 18
All in the Family
John Adams (father)–
John Quincy Adams (son)

George H. Bush (father)–
George W. Bush (son)

William H. Harrison
    (grandfather)–
Benjamin Harrison
    (grandson)

Page 18
Hysterical History
The Germans didn't bomb Pearl Harbor, the Japanese did (in 1941).

Page 19
Sister Sprinters
Four miles (They ran in opposite directions.)

Page 19
Sunrise, Sunset
The letter "t"

Page 20
Digestive Detective
When they went to the bathroom, Jeff noticed that Vinnie's urine was green (and smelly too!). Jeff's deductive reasoning told him that the source of the color was a recent experience with asparagus.

Page 20
3 Men and a Lady
Mr. George Washington, Mr. Andrew Jackson and Mr. Ulysses S. Grant are paper money. Her meal cost $71 with gratuity. Washington is on the $1 bill, Jackson is pictured on the $20 bill and Grant is on the $50 bill.

Page 21
Can You Canoe?
He doesn't exist. A grandfather, father and son got into the canoe and the son fell out, leaving the grandfather and the father… who is also a son.

Page 21
Hi Ho Silver
Friday was the name of Ben's horse.

Page 22
It's Not Over – Till it's Over
They were bowling and Andrew made two strikes in the 10th frame, putting him ahead by 23 points with one shot remaining. John doubted he could do better.

Page 22
Coin-cidentally
The Ag collection (Her nicknames come from the symbols on the Periodic Chart. Cu is copper, Ni is nickel and Ag is Silver.)

Page 23
Phractured Phrases
"What is good for the goose is good for the gander."
    —English proverb

"In this world nothing is certain but death and taxes."
    —Benjamin Franklin, letter to M. Leroy, 1789

"You're either part of the solution or part of the problem."
    —Eldridge Cleaver

"The only thing we have to fear is fear itself."
    —Franklin D. Roosevelt, Inaugural Address, 1933

Page 23
Road Trip
Sacramento, CA;
Columbus, OH;
Concord, NH;
Dover, DE

Page 24
Talking States
She died of Missouri. She wore her New Jersey. Ida no, but Alaska.

Page 24
Sheila the Great
Sheila was watching television.

217

Brainteasers

Page 25
Wait Until Dark
They were in Lapland, land of the midnight sun, and the sun didn't set until September.

Page 25
Nuts to You
1. Coconut
2. Doughnut
3. Cashew

Page 26
Drink Up
None (Singapore isn't in Thailand. You would go to the Raffles Hotel in Singapore.)

Page 26
A Bush in the Hand
White House lawn (Presidents Bush)

Page 27
Calendar Boy
Since all days have 24 hours, Jupiter reasoned that the rationale for specifying the number of hours in a day was to define what a day was. By his calculations, he had only used the limo 80 hours or three days and eight hours. He contended that he still had use of the limo for another 26 days and 16 hours.

Page 27
Sunny and Fair
Cher

Page 28
Down Under
South Australia is 18 hours ahead of California. They left on Tuesday at 3:00 p.m. California time and their flight took 15 hours total, so they arrived before they left.

Page 28
Double Trouble
Salem is the name of a US city in Massachusetts and Oregon. Portland is an incorrect answer since it does not have 17th-century architecture.

Page 29
Birthday Boy
He was born on February 29th. 1904 was the first leap year after 1896. Normally every four years there is a leap year, but there was no leap year in 1900.

Page 29
Shoe Who?
Sally's feet had swelled from the change in compression in the plane and the hours of sitting without getting proper circulation in her feet.

Page 30
Time to Go
She was just killing time while she waited for Mr. Rosner, her little lamb-chop.

Page 30
Friend or Fiend
Probably all three! Hyperbole is gross exaggeration, redundancy is repeating oneself and immaturity is always in character for Billy.

Page 31
Forgotten Children
Homer (Of course!)

Page 31
Epitome
The match

Page 32
Bus Stop
3 buses (Each bus holds 50 kids, so two buses hold 100 kids and the third is needed for the extra 25.)

Page 32
Happy Birthday, Granny
Claudia's father is 32 and his mother was 18 when he was born.

Page 33
Wide Load
Let air out of the tires (The truck will lower and be able to drive forward.)

Page 33
Compass Confusion
East (Los Angeles is actually east of Reno.)

Page 34
Cassie's Classic Conundrum

8	1	6
3	5	7
4	9	2

Page 34
Desperate Date
London
Berlin
Budapest
Paris

218

Brainteasers

Page 35
Phone Tree
45 individual conversations. The formula is $\frac{N(n-1)}{2}$, where N is the total number of kids. So $10(10-1) \div 2 = 45$. Another way to do it is to say Maia talked to nine, the next kid talked to eight and add up all the conversations.

Page 35
Fractional Sense
63 ($30 \div 1/2 = 60$,
       $60 + 3 = 63$)

100 (In base 5, the number 5 is 10, the number 15 is 20. To express 50, which is 10 groups of 5, the correct number is 100.)

Page 36
Busybody
She was a Justice of the Peace.

Page 36
Extra Credit
Edinburg and Sarajevo

Page 37
Chirp Chirp
They are all NFL team names.

Page 37
If I Ran the Zoo
Detroit, MI (home of the Detroit Tigers and the Detroit Lions)

Page 38
No Blankety Blanks
The <u>color</u> of the <u>ore</u> sent <u>Ken</u> and <u>Frank</u> on the wrong <u>road</u>.

<u>Bro</u>adway
<u>Ore</u>gon
<u>Ken</u>tucky
<u>Frank</u>fort
<u>Color</u>ado

Page 38
Time is Up
George (I only like things that end with the letter "e".)

Page 39
Life's Lessons
The letter "F"

Page 39
The Getaway
He's walking.

Page 40
Riddle Me This
A snake

Page 40
Exciting
I am an envelope.

Page 41
I'm Never Blue
A banana

Page 41
Who Was That Masked Man?
Because Elizabeth is playing baseball and the umpire calls her out!

Page 42
Weighing In
100 lbs.

Page 42
Roll Out the Barrel
Holes

Page 43
Sum-thing's Up
The digit is 1.
$11+1=12$

Page 43
Fur Sure
The outside, silly!

Page 44
Touching Allowed
Your lips

Page 44
Lonely Nights
It was full of married couples.

Page 45
Change of Heart
A lawsuit

Page 45
Time's Up!
It is 12:00. The hands of the clock are between the one and the two of 12.

Page 46
Freezer Burn
A Popsicle®

Page 46
SSSSSS
Prince…princes…princess

219

Symbol Simon

220

Symbol Simon

221

Secret Identities

222

Secret Identities

223

Armchair Puzzlers • Solutions

✶ About the Authors ✶

BOB MOOG co-founded University Games in 1985 and has been creating games, brainteasers, word puzzles and the like since childhood. He is the author of several other books, including *Gummy Bear Goes to Camp, 20 Questions, 30 Second Mysteries* and *Batty Brainteasers.*

AL SECKEL has published numerous award-winning books on the science of illusion and lectures at many of the world's most prestigious universities. He also builds interactive galleries on illusions and perception for science museums around the world.